CONNECTED BY THE LIGHT

John Elgaaen

Connected by The Light

Paranormal Experiences of a Psychic

Copyright © 2013 John Elgaaen.

All rights reserved. No part of this book may be used or reproduced by any means, graphic, electronic, or mechanical, including photocopying, recording, taping or by any information storage retrieval system without the written permission of the publisher except in the case of brief quotations embodied in critical articles and reviews.

Balboa Press books may be ordered through booksellers or by contacting:

Balboa Press
A Division of Hay House
1663 Liberty Drive
Bloomington, IN 47403
www.balboapress.com
1-(877) 407-4847

Because of the dynamic nature of the Internet, any web addresses or links contained in this book may have changed since publication and may no longer be valid. The views expressed in this work are solely those of the author and do not necessarily reflect the views of the publisher, and the publisher hereby disclaims any responsibility for them.

The author of this book does not dispense medical advice or prescribe the use of any technique as a form of treatment for physical, emotional, or medical problems without the advice of a physician, either directly or indirectly. The intent of the author is only to offer information of a general nature to help you in your quest for emotional and spiritual well-being. In the event you use any of the information in this book for yourself, which is your constitutional right, the author and the publisher assume no responsibility for your actions.

Certain stock imagery © Thinkstock.
Any people depicted in stock imagery provided by Thinkstock are models, and such images are being used for illustrative purposes only.

ISBN: 978-1-4525-7072-3 (e)
ISBN: 978-1-4525-7071-6 (sc)
ISBN: 978-1-4525-7073-0 (hc)

Library of Congress Control Number: 2013904891

Printed in the United States of America.

Balboa Press rev. date: 4/11/2013

To Dee
an amazing woman, perfect friend, and gift from spirit

Table of Contents

Acknowledgements ix

Preface xiii

Part I 1

   1   Psychic Beginnings 3
   2   The Magnificent Golden Light 14
   3   We Meet In Heaven 21
   4   Vision In The Night Sky 30
   5   Guardian Protects 36
   6   A Wonderful Beach Experience 43
   7   Nighttime Astral Trip 51
   8   Precognitive Event 61

Part II 73

   9   Before The Change 75
  10   The Change Arrives 83
  11   Angels Gather 92
  12   April 29th, 1992 101
  13   An Intuitive In Marin 109
  14   Light From The Other Side 116
  15   Dimness Of The Gray Plane 123
  16   Heaven's Close At Hand 130

Part III 141

  17   Sky Visitors 143
  18   A Place Called Paradise 151
  19   The Perfect Friend And Gift 163
  20   Ghost Girl Needing Help 170
  21   Spirit Communicates 177
  22   Someone At The Door 185
  23   Connecting With The Light 193

Epilogue 203

Acknowledgements

To all my family and friends behind the scenes:

I express my warmest appreciation for your positive support when beginning this calling, and during its creation and completion.

Especially To:

Joanne. You have been a bright ray of sunshine during this process. Thank you for your caring and upbeat enthusiasm.

Don. You have always been there for me with words of support. A sincere thank you for your genuine thoughtfulness.

Myriam. Your sensitive awareness is very strong and may it continue to grow. Thank you for your initial push.

Dee. You are a true blessing and gift from spirit. A most heartfelt thank you for displaying your goodness and light in my life.

Also Especially To:

All my friends and loved ones on The Other Side. I want to thank all of you for your guidance, being there for me, and sharing your creative energies of inspiration.

Most Especially To:

God. With deepest gratitude and humble appreciation for requesting through a male guide that I write this book. Thank you for giving me the opportunity.

Connected by The Light

Preface

Here on Earth, we live in a fascinating world of energies that not only surround us but are also within us everyday of our lives. When we view the fifth sense world of the earth plane, we can not directly see these forces with our physical eyes. However, we are able to indirectly observe them, witnessing the end result through a variety of means. These indirectly viewed energies take on many different forms, but they are always a life force that is here, being ever-present and in everything. Heat, electricity, sound, and wind are just a few of the many end results of these various types of energies.

From my experiences as a lifelong psychic and intuitive, I have repeatedly been shown the differences between the fifth sense world of energies here on Earth, and energies that exist beyond the physical earth plane. I have come to understand that first and foremost, each of us has a spiritual side that coexists with our physical body. It is our spiritual side that allows us to connect to different dimensions and energies that exist beyond our physical world.

Through countless extra sensory events, I have witnessed some of the spectacular beauty that exists in the high realms beyond Earth. I have also experienced the spiritual side right here on Earth, as well as various spiritual levels of the astral plane. This sixth sense world has been reached through a combination of paranormal means, such as "clear seeing," "clear knowing," and "clear sensing," all tools which are used to gain access and perception to our spiritual side.

One very important fact that has been constantly realized during these many personal psychic experiences is that each of us is multidimensional, and our spiritual side is capable of venturing out, reaching, and experiencing these other dimensions. We are so much more than simply humans living on Earth inhabiting a physical self, and our spiritual abilities to expand our extra sensory perceptions are quite limitless.

As you read about some of the many paranormal events I have had during my life, it is my hope that these occurrences will stir an inner aspiration within you to further expand your own personal awareness. You will discover the relationship I have between my physical and spiritual sides, and the connection that exists between the two. These paranormal events are written from my own perspective as a psychic and intuitive, and it is your decision to incorporate whatever you desire from these experiences into your own belief system and personal soul growth.

When reading about these different experiences, you will notice my constant intent and desire to maintain a strong spiritual connection with the high energy realms of light. It is the high realms of The Other Side that give us truth and purity, and for that reason, I have always felt the need to keep that link with those energies as strong as possible. The energies in those high places are perfect in every way, and they are filled with extremely high vibrations of unconditional love and caring. Tapping into some of these energies not only provides us with great positivity, but it also helps give us increased strength and abilities in coping with our challenges here on Earth.

It is an incredible universe beyond the physical earth plane. The spiritual side is captivating, and once we further strengthen our connection with that side of life, we will never want to be without that fortified bond. The high realms of light are filled with breathtaking colors and wonderful inspirational energies, all in an eternal atmosphere of endless joy and happiness. The people residing there live in a constant state of perfect harmony and bliss. It is my sincere wish that these personal psychic experiences will rouse your curiosity and interest, enabling you to further strengthen your own connection to the extraordinarily uplifting energies that exist on The Other Side.

PART I

1

Psychic Beginnings

Fascinating and sometimes astounding psychic experiences have been a central part of my life since a very young age. The first experience I can remember occurred around the age of six months. It was a warm late winter afternoon, and I was a tiny newborn infant having come into the world the previous summer. My birth the previous year was a joyous event for Mom and Dad, and they were now the proud parents of yet another son, the third one in the family. Just like other parents, they were thrilled by the new addition. Life was being good to them with a new child in the family, and they proudly displayed their pride and joy for all to see.

At that very young age, I consciously remember almost nothing about the first several years of life. However, there was one incident that has always stayed with me. That remembrance has never left and will always be stamped in my memory.

It was naptime that winter afternoon in Northern California, with every afternoon involving the same routine of putting me down to rest for a good nap. During one particular rest period, something very intriguing and stimulating happened. Even though there are no memories of the other afternoon naps, this one particular naptime has stayed in my consciousness as if it occurred yesterday. In fact, there are very few conscious memories of the first three years of life, but this one particular afternoon proved to be different.

As I quietly rested on the bed with stillness and silence in the room, suddenly my conscious awareness seemed to come alive. All of a sudden I could formulate thoughts in my mind and these thoughts were coming in the form of sentences. Where were they coming from and why was my awareness suddenly being stirred to life? I was a tiny infant that had six months earlier come into the world, so how could this be happening? Even more puzzling, these thoughts were in English, a language that I had not yet begun to learn. Why were the thoughts coming through in a language I did not know, and why was my conscious memory suddenly being awakened in this way? Lying on my back, I continued to study the surroundings, looking up at the walls and ceiling. Being so young at the time and unable to move my little body very much, I just kept staring at the features of the room from my location of the bed I was in.

This consciousness felt wonderful, suddenly being able to have thoughts rushing through my head. But why was this happening now, and why had it never happened before? Scanning the surroundings, I kept thinking to myself "Why are the colors in the room so dull, and where are the beautiful colors of Heaven?" These questions were strangely puzzling as my little infant eyes continued to study the room.

The curtains had been pulled to make it darker and easier to sleep, but the odd dullness in the room seemed to go beyond that. Although the room was darkened, the lack of depth to the colors seemed very strange and unusual to look at. "It's just so dull and dreary looking," were the constant thoughts rushing through my head. It was as if I had been used to incredibly vibrant colors and all of a sudden they were gone, having been replaced with bland tones that lacked intensity and had little depth. It was simply a room that lacked the vibrancy of Heaven. For those few minutes, I constantly looked around with great interest, all the while continuing to have thoughts in English.

After several minutes, a form suddenly appeared to the right side of me. It was a man, except this man was in spirit form. At the time, I didn't realize he was in a spiritual body, and as a tiny infant, I simply knew a person had appeared next to the crib. It was many years later thinking back on that day that it became obvious he was not in physical form.

Looking back on this event, I realized he had the normal features of an adult male, except with this particular male; there was one very important difference. There was light around him, a beautiful glowing light that seemed to radiate various shades of soft multicolor. After reaching older adolescent age thinking about this incident, I realized that is what made him so different from someone in a physical body. He radiated what I call "The Light." The warm and gentle light that emanated from him made him look almost transparent, when he suddenly appeared next to the bed, with all the colors of the rainbow softly being displayed around his body.

I was a tiny infant having a normal daytime rest period, when suddenly my consciousness was stirred with English sentences forming in my mind, and within a few minutes a man in spirit form quickly appeared to the right side of me. This man was in a definite rush, going past the bed in a fast and deliberate manner. As he went by, he telepathically spoke in English saying, "There is a fire. I am going to get help." His message was given to me by thought transference, and that is all he said. It was a bit hard to see him, since I was so tiny and unable to move my neck around to view him. After he had said those words with a certain amount of urgency, I watched him go past the bed, rapidly disappearing into the next room.

Many years later it was confirmed with Mom and Dad that

there was a small fire that had started right outside the house that afternoon. A babysitter was in the kitchen working during afternoon naptime, having the job of tending to me while they were out of the house. After the fire had started, she did discover it, quickly notifying the fire department to come and put it out. There was even a clipping in the local newspaper about the fire that had ignited that afternoon at my home.

After the man in spirit walked past my bedside, I suddenly lost conscious memory again. There is no recollection of the babysitter, the men from the fire department arriving, or my parent's upset over the incident. None of that can be remembered. There was a memory blank in my young life after that incident, similar to the void in memory a little while before the male in spirit had appeared. From that point forward, my conscious memory was once again gone until around the age of three or four. By that time, recall and consciousness started to rapidly develop.

That wonderful awareness and perception within me did come to life for a brief time on that late winter afternoon, but why did it happen at that time? Looking back upon the situation, it does seem the male in spirit form was acting as a protector and guardian, watching over the home and those inside. I strongly feel he went into the kitchen for the purpose of alerting the babysitter, influencing her thoughts and actions so that she would discover the fire that had started that afternoon.

I am an intuitive, having constantly experienced many forms of psychic phenomenon since this very young age. These events have always played a large and important role in my life. I want to share with you numerous spiritual experiences that I have had, and together we can look at these experiences, gaining more understanding and depth into the connection between the physical world and the world of the spiritual side.

Never judging any of these experiences, I just let them happen without logical reasoning, letting the time for rational analysis come after the event. Logical reasoning interferes with the psychic process, so when one of these sixth sense experiences occurs, it is important to just let it flow and happen naturally. It wasn't until numerous years after the event of the house fire and the male in spirit appearing, that I was able to rationalize what had happened. When it was occurring, I simply watched him, not realizing a psychic experience was taking place.

Why would a tiny infant wonder why the colors in that bedroom were so dull and lifeless? It is my belief that at such a young age we are still very familiar with the glorious colors of The Other Side. We are used to the energies and vibrancy of that dimension because we have just come from there. Each of us makes this journey between Heaven and Earth many times, with each trip back to Earth becoming yet another incarnation and lifetime. The fact that I was so young when questioning the dullness of the room, suggests the familiarity of Heaven was still with me and was fresh on my mind. The magnificent beauty and glory of The Other Side was in my memory, where all colors are infinitely more vibrant and beautiful than any here on Earth. I do feel that is why I questioned and felt very puzzled with the dull drabness of the colors in the room that day.

Why was a little newborn able to formulate thoughts into sentences and hear the male speak telepathically? It does seem impossible in a logical sense that an infant could do that. But once again, I think it has to do with the awareness of The Other Side. I had just come from a place that is very social and filled with people, a place where we telepathically communicate with each other and are always in spiritual form.

When the male in spirit rushed past me that afternoon, it became a very natural thing to see. I was simply witnessing something that was very familiar. The male in paranormal spirit form stirred my awareness, even though my perception had not yet been stimulated by the fifth sense earth dimension. I was way too young to have fully readapted to life in the physical realm. For that reason, my consciousness came to life when someone from the spiritual dimension came to help and warn in a time of danger.

We can be so thankful that there are those in spirit that watch over us and help guide us on our earthly path. This guardian spirit that came proved to do just that, coming to the aid of the babysitter and me. He was right there to help, giving assistance in a time of peril and risk.

Throughout my life, I have witnessed this type of help from the spiritual side of life, having seen this type of assistance happen over and over. They are here to help all of us whenever possible, and it is our privilege to try and develop a stronger connection with them. By the age of four, my earthly conscious memory was becoming fully developed, and I started to remember daily activities of life here on Earth. Up until that time, about the only conscious memory was of that one winter day when the small house fire ignited.

Another fascinating experience happened around the age of seven. It was the Christmas Season, a time of year that is so very special for children. There was a lot of joy and happiness in the air, and I was feeling the Christmas spirit like only a child can feel. Having a Christmas record and feeling very filled with the Christmas spirit, I decided to play it in the bedroom and listen to the music. Putting the record on the player, I hopped into bed feeling very excited about listening to the wonderful carols.

The music began to play and it sounded great. Although it sounded wonderful, I wanted to experience something more and to feel the music on a deeper level. Christmas is such a festive season, and I wanted to experience something very extraordinary. Much to my surprise, that is exactly what happened. While lying on the bed looking up at the ceiling listening to the carols, suddenly the room seemed to expand. It was as if the walls and ceiling were instantly gone, and the confines of the room had surprisingly expanded. Suddenly there was a feeling of total freedom and unlimited vistas, as I quietly stared at the world beyond my room.

My eyes seemed more glued to the scenery above me than to the sides where the walls had been. The ceiling was gone, and in its place were incredible sensations with an awareness that went far beyond Earth. There was a feeling of great unconditional love along with the visual effects of many beautiful colors. Next I heard amazingly splendid voices that sounded like those of angels, singing along with the carols. The pureness and great depth of their voices was unlike anything I had ever heard on Earth. As a child, I kept thinking that nothing here could ever sound like that. This amazing experience lasted for maybe ten minutes. During that time, I rested on the bed, staring up toward the ceiling experiencing Christmas in Heaven.

I have come to realize over the years that the feelings and awareness of the spiritual world are entirely different than the feelings of our physical earth plane. On The Other Side, all of the senses are hugely magnified, due to the pureness and high energies that exist in those realms. The elevated energies that exist there carry great goodness and purity. It is my sincere belief during that one evening as a little child listening to the Christmas music, a connection was made between Earth and Heaven. I was able to experience a portion of the true wonder of many heavenly voices singing with the music, giving praise to God. It was a wonderful experience, and the memories and feelings of the event will always stay with me.

It is such a special time when we are children growing up. We are constantly experiencing life, with so much to learn and so much living ahead of us. Other than numerous spiritual experiences, my very early childhood was a normal one. I enjoyed many of the activities young boys often enjoy doing, playing with friends and getting outside, anxiously ready to explore the world.

Infants and young children are some of the most psychic people since they have recently arrived back on Earth from The Other Side. They tend to experience things without logical reasoning and analysis, just letting it happen and not questioning why it is occurring. It is only a few years later after much conditioning of life here on Earth that children start to get older and begin to loose this natural ability to tune into the sixth sense world. Adults very often tell them that their imaginary friends are just figments of their imagination, insisting that they need to stop their imagining and get back to the real world. So the conditioning of daily life and the breaking away from spiritual awareness normally gets stronger, with the connection between the physical and spiritual sides gradually becoming weaker. Eventually, most older children and adolescents have pretty much broken away from their strong connection with the sixth sense realm, having their thoughts and concentration devoted to life in the physical world.

Growing up as a child, I had more than my share of psychic awareness around me. I seemed to be a little different from most children, because I was refusing to break away from spiritual sixth sense awareness. During this time, I kept trying to concentrate more on the physical world, but this other world of magnified senses was there as well, and it refused to leave. Being only a child, I had no idea what it was, and that it can actually be very helpful to us. I didn't understand that the high energies radiating from Heaven can help us in so many ways. Without this understanding, it became very confusing at times, because it was just there and would not go away.

Constantly seeing and knowing things, it became very baffling as I realized others didn't see and know what I was experiencing. Images would flash in front of me while at other times there was just this "knowing" about people and things. It was all such a mystery to my young mind, and by the ages of eight and nine, all I wanted to do was to try and block it out. Whatever this was around me, I just wanted to be a normal boy growing up like other children. Experiencing life in both the physical and spiritual worlds was perplexing, and being only a child, I had never heard of psychic phenomenon and sixth sense awareness.

During this time it seemed there was no one to talk to, and the other older children didn't seem to have as much of this awareness. For that reason, I kept the thoughts of what I was experiencing to myself in the hopes this perplexing situation would somehow go away. Now getting older, I was growing up in a physical world and wanted to experience only that world. As a boy getting older, I certainly didn't care about this other paranormal world. It was interfering with my young life, and it felt like it was time to just be a boy, putting this other world aside.

One day around the age of nine, I was in the garage playing and having fun like children will have, when suddenly a male in spirit appeared. He must have been about ten feet away and was looking directly at me with great interest, while I looked right back at him with equal fascination. We both silently stood looking at one another while he made no attempt to telepathically communicate any type of message. As we studied each other, I noticed the same quality around him that had been around the male spirit numerous years earlier as an infant. His body also appeared to be composed of light. It was not a physical body, but rather a body of energies that emitted various shades and colors. At the time, I was not aware of his clothing, being too busy observing and studying the fascinating glowing colors that surrounded him. During this entire time, I never sensed any communication from him.

Seeing the male in spirit as an infant had given me great comfort. It was something perfectly normal and natural to see, since I was freshly familiar with life on The Other Side. However, now being older and seeing this other male in spirit form was confusing, since I was increasingly becoming more conditioned to the physical side of life here on Earth.

My family is religious and did go to church regularly, but that was different than this world I was experiencing. That was a physical church with physical people coming together to worship. However, the spiritual world I seemed to have contact with was not like that. I noticed that although a person could not touch the spiritual side with their physical hands, it was obvious through my perceptions that it was still very real and just as real as anything on Earth. There was no one around to share those thoughts with at that young age, and there was no one to tell about the experience of the male in the garage. If only there had been someone in physical form to share the experience with, and they could have explained to my young mind that it's ok to sense and see these things. It would have been very gratifying if someone had been there to say that the sixth sense world can be a normal part of our life here on Earth, and that the understanding of the spiritual side can play a very important role.

After that experience, I had witnessed and sensed enough of the world beyond the physical. It would have been great to have shared these experiences with others, but it seemed there was no one around me that could see or feel these things in the same way I did. For that reason, I just wanted to be like the other children, and devote my childhood time to growing up in the physical world.

After viewing the male in the garage, I ran off into the house. While in the house, I said a little prayer asking God to please take some of this awareness away from me, so I wouldn't see people in spirit anymore. Becoming more conditioned to life on Earth, I was too young to fully understand it, and it was getting too difficult to experience.

God did answer that special request. The experiences slowed

down to a trickle, and I was very jubilant about that fact. Now it was possible to simply be a boy, being like the other children who had already lost most of their psychic awareness with the spiritual side of life, due to their advancing age.

The sixth sense experiences were much more subdued until the age of seventeen. It was nice to simply be a growing adolescent, forgetting about the paranormal awareness that had been so prominent years earlier. However, at seventeen years old, the sixth sense events started to once again increase. But things were different now, and being much older, I was more capable of dealing with what was being experienced. At this older age, it was possible to experience psychic events, think about them afterwards, and then come to a further understanding of what had occurred and why.

God did fulfill my request as a boy of nine, waiting until a time when I was grown up enough to more fully understand. It would have been rewarding if there had been a person to coach and help me as a child, explaining what was happening and what paranormal events were. But since there was no one, and no one even knew about this personal awareness and sensitivity, it was God's blessing that the connection had quieted until that older age. At the age of seventeen, my psychic awareness was going to reactivate in a major way.

2

The Magnificent Golden Light

As my school friend and I sat discussing various topics, I quickly said, "How awesome it is to be seventeen. There are so many things to do now that we are practically adults." Seventeen is a very magical age. At that time of life, there is very often some confusion whether we are grown up adolescents, or whether we have suddenly become young adults. We are in a type of metamorphosis, transforming from childhood into adulthood. But despite some confusion regarding our growing up process, most of us at that age still desire to feel we have become quite grown up, being more of an adult than an adolescent.

My life at seventeen was a good one, with another year of high school still remaining. It was gratifying to be in the third year, enjoying the many perks and advantages of an upperclassman. Living in the San Francisco Bay Area at the time, it seemed there was always plenty to do and many activities to participate in. The sixth sense awareness and sensitivity that had been with me during the earlier childhood years was remaining fairly subdued. I still had a certain degree of psychic awareness within me, but it seemed life in the physical sense was taking a stronger hold. Enjoying the moment seemed much more important at this age than thinking about spiritual experiences and making a connection with The Other Side.

Although I was taking great pleasure in living the active life of a seventeen year old in the physical world, a major change was about to commence. Many years earlier as a child of nine, I had asked God to please take away some of the psychic awareness and sensitivity within me. It had been too difficult for a young boy of that age to understand. My simple short prayer at the age of nine was answered, and the sixth sense connection was greatly lessened. Although those memories of earlier childhood days were neatly stored away in my mind, I never gave them much thought at the time. It was much more fun just being seventeen and enjoying daily life in the physical fifth sense way.

One night all of that changed, and I once again became very aware of the connection between the physical and spiritual worlds. From that time, the psychic awareness increased, permanently staying with me from that point forward. Night came and it was time to get to bed. Hopping into bed, I planned for a good night's sleep, not really thinking about much except some of the school activities coming up the next day. Little did I realize on that particular night, an important paranormal event would occur that would leave an immense and lasting impression.

After drifting off to sleep, I was soon in a deep restful slumber. What happened next came totally by surprise and without warning. A male in spirit suddenly appeared next to my spiritual self as I slept. My spiritual body was on the astral plane; a plane of existence that I feel is between our earth plane and The Other Side. It is a place where we can go to meet people on an astral level, conversing with them and telepathically discussing situations or events that are relevant to our lives. In addition to meeting up with friends and loved ones, we also go to the astral plane during sleep to try and solve problems of everyday life on Earth. For those reasons, I like to call the astral plane the communication and problem solving plane.

The male standing beside me spoke and simply said, "You are going to find out what is at the end of infinity." What an amazing and astonishing thing for him to say. At the time, I kept thinking to myself "What does he mean and what is he talking about?" Although I was feeling rather confused in what he had said, there was also a feeling of enthrallment and awe in his comment.

Over the years since that time, I have come to learn the difference between mere problem solving on the astral plane and the more powerful spiritual experiences and messages. There is a different feel to each. Problem solving usually has a storyline in the form of a dream, having a beginning, middle, and ending. However, when an important message is given on the astral level, normally it is quite short and to the point. Although the actual paranormal experience can sometimes be rather long, messages are usually quite short.

I am not sure why it happens this way, but my theory is that it takes quite a bit of energy to communicate the message to us, and for that reason messages are normally brief. There is also the fact that the person in spirit has come for a definitive purpose and wants to be very straight forward, giving the communication in a very concise and to the point manner. For those reasons, when I receive a message from someone in spirit, it is normally a one or two line communication.

After the male guide had given the message, he continued to stay right at my side and did not leave. Immediately, I found both of us standing stationary in some type of tunnel. Though clairsentience, also known as "clear feeling," I could sense he was taking me somewhere. Why was this happening and where were we going? Although this tunnel was a mystery, I felt strangely excited with anticipation of what was about to happen.

The tunnel was neither large nor small, but it was just large enough to be in without feeling claustrophobic. As with all tubes, the interior was perfectly rounded and formed a circular floor, wall, and ceiling around us. Suddenly we were on the move being propelled forward through this fascinating tunnel. As we started to proceed forward, I noticed light starting to appear on the interior circular walls. The light was composed of all the colors of the rainbow in wonderful hues of reds, yellows, greens, and blues. It was an awesome and beautiful sight to observe these colors as we started to move ever faster inside the tunnel of light. The faster we moved through the tunnel, the faster the breathtaking colors started to rush past us. Soon we were moving very fast, with the colors starting to streak and beginning to blend together with one another.

Another interesting quality that took place was the sound inside the tunnel. It sounded very similar to a jet engine taking off on the runway. The faster we went, the faster the streaks of color whizzed by us, and the louder the jet engine sound became. The fascinating sound of the jet engine started with a lower hum, getting higher-pitched and more intense as we proceeded ever faster. This intriguing experience was not only fascinating, but it was also totally astounding. Not feeling any sense of danger or fright, I was happily going along for the ride, anxious to see what would happen next. The ever increasing speed and shrill sound continued for a short while, as I continued to observe the colors now hurtling past us at a very fast rate.

Now advancing through the circular tunnel at an incredibly fast speed, I noticed the various hues of colors start to merge into one. As they merged together, a beautiful white coloring started to replace the individual colors. I was speechless watching this process unfold, and the male guide said nothing at the time as we propelled through the tunnel of white light. How fast were we going? Although I had no idea at the time, it was visually obvious as we shot through the tunnel at lightning speed that we were going astoundingly fast.

After this process of propelling faster and faster, we finally reached our maximum speed. It became a crescendo of speed and sound as we zoomed through the tunnel of brilliant white light with the jet engine noise rattling in my ears. Even though the noise was loud and high pitched, it didn't hurt my ears. Rather, the sound was actually beautiful in its own way. It was a sixth sense sound that is not heard on the earth plane in a normal fifth sense way. The male guide had said I would find out what is at the end of infinity, and now we were going at full speed through the tunnel of light toward something. This tunnel had been a multitude of colors but was now a tunnel of pure white light. What is at the end of forever, and what were we heading toward? It was all so baffling.

I have often thought many times about this experience over the years and have wondered how fast we were moving. My guess is that we either started at the speed of light when we first started to propel forward, or that we entered the speed of light when the colors in the tunnel turned into brilliant white. Nothing here on Earth could ever compare to the speed that the male guide and I traveled during that experience.

After what felt to be several minutes of maximum speed, I suddenly sensed something ahead of us. It was a feeling and a knowing, also called clairsentience and Clair cognizance in paranormal terminology. Clairsentience is the ability to physically or emotionally feel sixth sense experiences, while Clair cognizance is the ability to know things that are not logically possible to know in a fifth sense way. As the guide and I continued to advance forward through the tunnel, I knew for a fact and without a doubt something magnificent was directly ahead of us. The energy we were moving toward could literally be felt in my entire being.

How can clairsentience and Clair cognizance be described?

Most sixth sense awareness is difficult to put into words simply because there are no sensations on the physical earth plane that are comparable. Although a bit hard to describe, it felt as if my soul, which is the essence of our spiritual self, was being drawn and pulled into something very great and powerful. There was a knowing within me, and there was no doubt that whatever this astonishing energy was, we were getting very close to it. The full throttle speed and high pitched jet engine sound had been with us for awhile. However, at this time, both the speed and sound started to dissipate. The speed did not slow in movement, nor did the sound lower in volume. Rather, the speed and sound simply dissolved and dissipated as we entered into this new energy space.

Suddenly the glorious white light of the tunnel was gone and the sound was silent. We had entered a new place, finding ourselves in a total expanse of golden light. The only thing that could be seen was gold, the most amazing pure golden hue imaginable. It was so intense and so breathtaking, I am positive I was only experiencing a very minute portion of its true magnificence.

As a psychic and sensitive, I always just let the experience happen without trying to logically explain it at the time. Analysis and examination can come later, after the event has occurred. Looking back upon the event, it is my sincere belief that the male guide and I had entered God's home, the place where the God energy resides. The tunnel of light was used as a means of transport to reach this light of gold. It reminded me of a room completely filled with the most breathtaking gold coloring possible, but of course it was infinitely much more. The God Light is energy of such brilliant and high elevation, that it emits a pure golden light. Within this light are the thoughts and feelings of an incredible intelligence, a force so breathtaking and all-knowing that is always watching over every one of us.

The energy in that space felt like some incredible super

computer. In addition to the sensation of great knowledge within the light, there was also a great depth of emotion, with feelings of both happiness and sadness. I did feel through clairsentience that the intelligent residing within that light is very happy when those on Earth are good, but greatly saddened when we are not. Whatever you envision God to be and whatever your belief system is, it is possible for all of us to reach out to that magnificent light of gold.

On that night at the age of seventeen, it was revealed through this personal experience what is at the end of forever. According to the amazing occurrence, it is the God energy. My guide had transported me from the astral plane to the high rarified energies of this golden light. The paranormal experience that night became the very moment that reopened much of my spiritual awareness and sensitivity. It was an awareness that had been more subdued and silent since the age of nine, but now it was back. At seventeen, I was now older and better able to start experiencing these events, without the confusion of a young nine year old mind. It had been planned this way for my life, and it was now time for me to once again further strengthen my light connection with The Other Side.

3

We Meet In Heaven

After the golden light occurrence the previous year, it seemed my awareness of the higher realms of The Other Side had increased considerably. The energies from that light had apparently stirred my sensitivities, awakening them and bringing them back to life. Many people think a spiritual sign must always come through in a form like Gabriel blowing his horn. However, most of the time that is not the case. There are occasions when one of these communications will come through very loud and clear, in an explicit manner like a clap of thunder. But as a rule it doesn't have to happen that way. Communications and signs very often come through in a softer and gentler manner.

The higher energies of the spiritual side will very often show themselves to us in this gentler way. They are being sent from a place that has a much higher vibration than here on Earth. For that reason, communication from those high places will very often be more subdued. However, since those energies are much more elevated than ours here on Earth, they do tend to come through to us quite fast and fleeting.

The people in the higher realms live in a world of light energy. They live life in a very real body, but their bodies are in spiritual

21

form, not the denser and heavier physical bodies we have here on Earth. The energies of light where they live have a wonderful feeling of constant unconditional love which permeates everything there. They are in a place that is eternally warm and kindhearted, where every person genuinely cares for everyone else.

When tuning into this amazing world, we must place our thoughts on these high energies and nothing less. It's the high vibrations that will give us better understanding and perception, so we must feel pureness of heart and an unconditional feeling of caring for others when reaching out to these realms. Trying to incorporate these qualities into our thinking will help us connect better with those high places. In addition to the high realms of light, there are also lower energies on the spiritual side. This is why we must only strive for the very highest of energies, and as long as we do that, we will hopefully start to achieve a stronger connection with The Light.

After about one year following the tunnel and golden light experience, another important occurrence was about to happen. I have noticed over the years that each experience can be entirely different from each other, with no two paranormal events being exactly alike. Those in spirit do indeed have many ways to communicate with us, and they are always finding new and unusual ways.

One day I had a clairsentient feeling there was some type of message from a group of people on The Other Side that needed to come through, but I didn't know what the message was or how to access it. These feelings continued during the day with a constant urging within me to somehow receive that communication from them. It felt like they were continuously trying to pull me toward them.

Each of us receives feelings during our everyday life. Maybe it's a feeling your boss will be upset and that turns out to be the case, or a feeling you are going to have a good day and it does happen. This was a similar type of feeling; except it was a sixth sense clairsentient feeling involving those on The Other Side. In fact, it was possible to clairvoyantly see them with my third eye vision. Clairvoyance is the paranormal ability to see with our mental third eye, which is located in our head between and slightly above our eyes. It is an energy chakra center, and when open, allows us to mentally see a psychic picture or image in our mind's eye. Not only could I feel them trying to pull me toward them, but it was also possible to see them as well. There was a small group of them, and I had a feeling deep within me it was important to meet up with them. Now that I knew what they requested of me, how was I going to find a way so we could get together?

Suddenly the same day after having received the initial impression to meet with them, I developed an earache. The earache had come on suddenly, and it had not been there prior to that day. However, now it was very much there, and the right ear was hurting. It did seem a bit odd that this ear problem would abruptly come out of the blue, but due to the fact it was bothering a great deal, I had to try and do something to remedy the problem.

While driving to San Francisco that afternoon, I stopped in Berkeley at a phone booth to look up an ear doctor for the problem. During this time, I continued to feel the compelling urge to get together with those in spirit. They were constantly sending this clairsentient feeling as I continued having the earache. They wanted me for some reason, and I was going to try and fulfill their wish.

There was an ear doctor in that area and after driving to his office, I quickly walked inside. He was able to see me right away and after the usual paperwork, he took me into a room and pointed to the patient chair. After getting settled in the chair, he began looking into my ears with his light scope. First he looked into one ear and then the other. While he was doing this, I suddenly felt faint, and then started to pass out. The room started to fade out and darken, while I tried my best to maintain consciousness and composure.

However, it was hopeless, and I quickly blacked out with my limp body quietly resting in the patient's recliner chair. Immediately after passing out, I saw a small group of people in spirit standing in a circle directly around and above me. For a few brief moments, I looked up at them with a feeling of puzzlement and surprise, as they looked down at me with warmhearted and glowing smiles.

In the proverbial twinkling of an eye, my spiritual body was instantly standing alongside of them. It was an astonishing experience to go from the earth plane to that higher plane, as I felt no movement of my spirit going from one place to the next. Rather, it happened in an instant. One moment my spiritual self was with my physical body, and the next instant I was standing next to these caring people.

After the instant transition of moving from the earth plane to that dimension, something else happened that was very fascinating. An immediate shift of consciousness occurred within me which was greatly felt the moment I arrived on that high plane of existence. It was a wonderful sensation as I shifted from the lower awareness and sensitivity of the earth plane to a higher realm that has much greater sensitivity and depth. The instant after arriving there, my spiritual body was overflowing with great aliveness, contentment, and peace.

When entering that beautiful atmosphere, the feeling of instant recognition and higher consciousness totally enveloped my entire being. I was very familiar with that dimension and had actually returned back home to the place we call Heaven, which is on The Other Side. Feeling a great inner joy that remained constant, the delight and feeling of wholesomeness within me was overflowing. My friends in spirit and I had been reunited with each other, and all of us very much wanted to converse.

There were about five or six people, both male and female, within the group. We started to excitedly talk with each other, all of us having facial features and emotions of great happiness now that we were together. I was feeling extremely upbeat and full of enthusiasm with the incredible feeling of warmth and caring found within this higher realm. There was no negativity in that wonderful place, and everything within that dimension was eternally perfect. Each of us had total unconditional love and genuine compassion for one another.

Another feature that stood out as we talked was the youthfulness of the group in spirit. While studying their facial features, I noticed they had no wrinkles, appearing very young looking and in their prime. Their faces were vibrant and glowing with a soft radiance, and they looked to be about thirty years old. Did I also become a thirty year old with no wrinkles when arriving there, since I was only eighteen years old at the time? It was impossible to say for sure since there were no mirrors and therefore not possible for me to see my own face. However, it does seem highly probable I had also been transformed into an eternally young thirty years old after entering that dimension. I was in a realm with an extremely high energy level and being in spiritual form, I most likely also appeared like them.

These people, although in spirit, still had very real bodies. They were not wisps of vapor floating around meeting together in a group. Rather, they had distinct bodies with definitive body features. Being composed of the lighter and higher energies of The Other Side, they looked like people here except for their eternally young thirty year old appearance. Just like on Earth, some of the people in the group were heavier and some were thinner, some taller and some shorter. But they were very real people with very real bodies, and because of the high energies of that dimension, their body features were amazingly youthful.

What did the surroundings look like during this visit to Heaven? Although there have been other times in my life that I have had glimpses of Heaven's beautiful surroundings, this time nothing could be seen in the background. Apparently the important part of this journey was the actual meeting up with these people. Any background scenery was unimportant and therefore not seen. During the entire time of the visit, I only noticed the group of people and the qualities they displayed.

We chatted for what felt like quite a long time, possibly forty-five minutes or longer. During this time, I continued to study the features of those in the group. My attention was constantly drawn to the remarkable unconditional caring that I felt from their hearts. It was amazing to sense such genuine empathy among the group, and they were certainly my loved ones and friends that had wanted to meet with me. That type of caring is very rare here on Earth, and yet there is it perpetually commonplace and ever-present.

What did we talk about during that lengthy visit? Unfortunately, I can not remember much about our actual discussion. It might seem strange that so much can be remembered about the experience, and yet it is so difficult to remember what we talked about. There is most likely a reason for this amnesia that needs explaining. I do sense that our discussion had a lot to do with my life here on Earth. We were meeting up for an important reason, not to just have some casual chitchat on The Other Side. Rather, there was something very urgent to discuss during our reunion, and that is why they had called me to Heaven.

Spiritual laws are very different from the laws here on Earth. A heavenly type of code of ethics is a major part of law there and plays a very important role. From my understanding as a psychic, I do believe we come to Earth to experience and hopefully overcome negativity. Earth is our classroom, and we are here to learn, hopefully furthering our soul growth for the glory of God. There was something very important that day for the group of loved ones to discuss with me. However, if I had come back to the earth plane with the knowledge we had discussed, that might have hindered my hoped for soul growth in this lifetime. For that reason, the natural spiritual code of ethics law that is in place there kicked in. Why should I be given some of the answers to various parts of my life, when it is up to me to work with situations and find those answers for myself? Because of that fact, the amnesia of what was said automatically activated after coming back to Earth. There is a reason why I can not consciously remember what we discussed, but there is also an important reason why we had that meeting.

After what felt like a long discussion, we bid our heavenly farewells and in an instant, my spiritual self was back in my physical body. After coming to from the fainting spell, I noticed the doctor and his assistant were anxiously bringing me back to consciousness. I quickly asked the ear doctor "How long did I pass out?" His brief reply was "A couple of seconds."

Of course I said nothing to the doctor and his assistant about the amazing event that had just been experienced. In fact, I never told anyone about it afterward. After the doctor's comment that I had only passed out a couple of seconds, I began to think about the time factor in Heaven. It did seem intriguing that the people in spirit and I could chat for such a long time, and yet in Earth time, it was only a matter of seconds. From my perspective as a psychic, both time and space on The Other Side are very different from time and space here on Earth. In fact, they are so different; it is quite difficult for us here to comprehend the concepts.

Time in Heaven is eternal and is without a past, present, or future like here on Earth. It's as if time there were only measured in the moment and by event. They can view the life charts of those here on Earth, but a life chart having a past, present, and future is something that is only experienced on the earth plane. The concept of eternal life explains why I was able to have a forty-five minute or longer conversation with them, and yet the actual length of time here on Earth during the visit was a mere couple of seconds.

I will most likely always have a hard time grasping that time concept while being here on Earth, but Heaven is eternal, and time there is much different than here. Interestingly, while I was there in the everlasting moment, I felt very comfortable with that time, having it seem perfectly normal and a well understood part of life there. It is only here on the earth plane where the concept is hard to understand.

Space is also very different there, and this concept is a little easier for me to understand. Simply put, it is possible to fit a large number of people and surroundings into a very small space, which of course is totally different than life on Earth. Although people and surroundings here take up physical space, the spiritual side is not in physical form. There is no limitation regarding space. For that reason, space there is altered to fit the needs of the people and surroundings.

I do believe through personal observation and experience that Heaven is a mere several feet above us. Immediately after passing out, I saw my friends and loved ones surrounding me three or four feet above my body. From my observation during numerous other instances, Heaven is actually a dimension that is literally right on top of us. Through various paranormal experiences, I have seen Heaven to be a plane of existence that is not out in space or on a cloud somewhere, but rather right here superimposed directly above our own dimension. Although it is right here on top of us, it is worlds apart in vibration. Their vibration runs much faster and higher than ours here on Earth. In order to create a stronger connection with that world, we must put pureness of thought into our hearts as we reach out to that dimension. The high energy world directly above us is a world free of negativity, so we must concentrate on goodness and purity, which will help to raise our own energies and strengthen our connection with that side.

It is very astonishing that I would meet a couple of the people in the group that day many years later here on Earth. At the time of this heavenly visit, I did not yet know them on the earth plane. We are both physical and spiritual beings while living on Earth, with all of us having a spiritual side. With time being eternal on that plane, those loved ones that I had not yet met on Earth were able to have their spiritual side attend the heavenly visit. We are multidimensional beings and capable of spiritual travel between dimensions.

After coming to from the fainting spell and regaining my composure, I paid the bill and left the doctor's office. He never found anything wrong with the ears, and I was never bothered with them after that doctor visit. Spirit had indeed found a way to reach out to me, having me be present at that very important talk we had that day. It would have been nice to have consciously remembered what we had talked about on that very special occasion. However, apparently spiritual law would not allow it, with the many learning experiences of Earth life positioned directly ahead for a young eighteen year old man.

4

Vision In The Night Sky

There are plentiful ways spirit can communicate messages to us. During my life, I have found that those residing in the high energies of The Other Side wish to form a bond with us here on earth, many times sending signs in rather unusual ways. Signs can occur quite often, and we only need to search for them. After discovering a sign, we can try to understand what the meaning might be. Communication from loved ones and kindred friends in Heaven can come in such forms as thought impression, visions, thought impression clairaudience, and other types of sixth sense phenomenon. But messages don't have to be in those methods, and spirit will often send signs in other ways as well.

A sign that is sent might be something as simple as an out of season bird in winter, suddenly appearing out of the blue perched on your porch railing. Or suddenly a pleasant warm feeling comes across you in the middle of having a real unpleasant day. It could be a thought to buy a certain item, and when your birthday arrives, you are given just the type of item you had wanted to purchase. Or a sign could be when you are having an emotionally down day, and suddenly you receive an unexpected phone call from a friend you haven't heard from in ages, bringing you a lot of joy and uplifting your mood. There are so many ways spirit can speak to us. The people and loved ones on The Other Side want a strong connection with us, helping us during difficult times and being there for us throughout our lives. They desire to communicate various thoughts and ideas to us, being our lifelong spiritual companions.

One type of sign from the spiritual side is the vision. Visions have been experienced and recorded by all types of people throughout the ages. But just what is a vision? From my personal experience, I feel a vision is something that is seen with the physical eyes but is not there in the physical sense. It is something that appears physical but is instead spiritual.

People under the influence of a substance sometimes say they have had a vision. But that type of vision is different from the high energy spiritual vision. They are very possibly tuning into the spiritual side while under the influence, but they are most likely not tuning into the higher realms. Rather, they are very likely receiving the vision from a lower spiritual level. It is very important when looking into the spiritual side that we always aim for the highest possible energies, only tuning into The Light and nothing else. The very high vibrations emanating from The Light are always filled with all things good and pure, which provide us with truth and honesty.

From my experiences, a vision is shown when there is a need to make a specific point or to forewarn. It is a very useful communicative tool often used by spirit, and is yet another way they can get their message across to us. When I am being shown a vision, I am actually seeing it with my physical eyes and normally during the experience, fail to realize it is coming in from the spiritual side. It is so real when it is occurring, often I will not realize it's a vision until afterward. Because of this fact, I never overanalyze a psychic vision until it is over with. After it has been experienced, it is then possible to start thinking more about it, beginning to rationalize what has just happened.

One such vision occurred during my teenage years, being only eighteen years old at the time. My family and I were close friends with an elderly gentleman that lived in a beautiful resort area of California called Lake County. We would often go up to vacation in that county and stay in a cabin close to his house. Over the years we got to know him quite well and became good friends with him.

He was a man of fine character and enjoyed chatting about many things. His favorite discussion was talking about the once in a lifetime trip he took, driving back to the hills of Kentucky and visiting with relatives. Whenever we would go up to Lake County on vacation, we would always find something to talk about with Frank. Having lost his wife to age related problems, he was now living by himself. Yet he always had a smile on his face and a kind word to say.

"That was the best trip of my life," Frank proudly announced about his cross country road trip. "I've always wanted to make that trip, and I'm sure glad I took it," he said with a great amount of zeal. "Have you done any fishing lately?" I asked, knowing that would stir a lot of enthusiasm in him. He replied with a quick "Oh yes, I caught some good sized bluegills and a catfish." This is the type of discussion we often had with him, and we always looked forward to our visits together.

As the years passed, Frank's health started to gradually deteriorate. Finally it got to a point his physical health was no longer very good. Dad would often call up to Lake County and talk with the person watching over him. As the days and weeks passed, I would often ask Dad how Frank was doing health wise. His reply was always about the same, "He's not doing so well, but he's hanging on."

It was during that time of Frank's poor physical health that I started saying a short simple prayer. I simply said, "God, please give me a sign when Frank passes." That short little request was often made during the weeks that followed. Looking back on that situation, I am not really sure why I was making that request. It was possibly due to the fact we were all concerned about him, and I simply wanted to know when he was no longer with us in the physical sense. Maybe I was even hoping that after being shown a sign of his departure, I would be able to sense his spirit after he was gone, still feeling his presence. Dad continued to periodically call up to Lake County; finding out about Frank's latest health status. During that time, I continued to say my short little prayer, asking for some type of sign when Frank had passed. It seemed I wanted to know the instant he was gone.

Additional time passed. As even more weeks went by, he was very often on my mind and in my thoughts. Finally one night around 9 or 10 p.m. something very unusual happened. I was outside at the time, when without any type of forewarning, suddenly part of the sky turned red. It was late enough at night; there was no longer any remaining light from the sun that had set. The sky was completely darkened, and the setting sun had totally given way to the nocturnal sky. However, instantly that was not the case, and a portion of the sky was now red, leaving me feeling very puzzled and perplexed.

Looking to the south and studying this very strange occurrence, I couldn't understand how a large portion of the sky could appear red, with the remaining portion continuing to be dark as night. It was so odd to see, and at the time I wondered if there was a large fire in the vicinity. But that theory made no sense since the reddish hue took up one complete part of the sky with the separation between the red and the night sky appearing in a straight line. "What a fascinating, yet puzzling thing to view," I kept thinking to myself. There was no variation in the red coloring. It was constant, and it was almost like looking at a red sheet of paper placed up in the dark sky.

This was not possible in a logical fifth sense way, but I didn't think of that fact as I continued to view this strange occurrence with interest. At the time, it never occurred to me that the mysterious reddish sky that night was actually a vision taking place. Visions are often so real for me when they are occurring, I can not tell the difference between seeing something in the fifth sense way and experiencing something that is sixth sense coming in from the spiritual realms.

Simply experiencing the moment, I was not thinking that the strange red coloring was totally illogical in a physical way. My initial thought was that it was indeed happening on a physical level and was a perfectly natural event, that somehow the red coloring in the sky was normal with a standard explanation. So I just watched it, letting the occurrence unfold, never over rationalizing the event until it was over with. It was only afterward that a logical conclusion was made that it was indeed a vision.

This extraordinary red sky continued for possibly several minutes at most, although being so intrigued with what has happening, I did loose some track of time. Watching the mysterious sky for fifteen or twenty seconds, I would then turn my eyes away, thinking it might be gone when I once again looked at the sky. Repeatedly I did this, turning my eyes away and then looking back. But it didn't go away and instead remained constant. Finally after what felt like several minutes, it suddenly disappeared and was gone. During the following days after that odd event, I came to realize it was a vision. A spiritual sign had occurred that evening, and yet it looked so physically real in a fifth sense way at the time.

The same night a portion of the sky turned red over my home, our good friend Frank up in Lake County passed from this world to The Other Side. It was days after his passing that we called up to Lake County, finding out what had happened and being told of the news. God had indeed answered my short simple prayer. I had asked for a sign when it was Frank's time to depart, and a sign in the form of a vision was certainly given. The sixth sense world is an amazing world, and it is open to all of us. There are so many ways for that world to communicate with us. But we must always try our very best to approach spirituality with pureness of heart. It's that pureness that will help strengthen the connection between this world and The Light of The Other Side.

5

Guardian Protects

While quickly driving from the campus to a local movie theatre with my friend, I enthusiastically said, "College is really terrific." It really was a fun time of life, and I was totally enjoying every minute of it. The daily adventure and excitement of college life was constant. Not only was it a time of learning and developing as a young adult, but there was also a great feeling of freedom and release that many of us shared during this time of our lives. There was no one to dictate our lifestyle, and it was up to each person to study and mentally thrive as much as we wanted. College life involved a lot of serious, disciplined study habits, and if those habits were not met, we would suffer with our grades. However, there was still ample time for extracurricular activities, exploring and enjoying the world around us like never before.

The school I attended was in Southern California, just south of Los Angeles. The campus and area around the college had a small town feel, despite the fact it was in a good sized city within a huge metropolitan area. For that reason, the small town atmosphere gave the campus a very personalized mood.

At the time, I had two aunts and two uncles living in the San Fernando Valley just north of Los Angeles. On some weekends I would drive up to see them, taking the drive of forty minutes if traffic was light and spending some time with one of them. They were always delighted to see me and would constantly greet me with warmhearted smiles on their faces. Normally I would alternate visits between the two aunts and uncles, staying with one set on one visit and the other aunt and uncle the next time.

One weekend I made the usual journey up to see them and spent the night with Mildred and Don. As usual, my aunt would come to the door with a warm greeting and lots of friendly hospitality. After I went inside, she would quickly say that she would be preparing some food a bit later, which of course was very pleasing to hear after being quite tired of cafeteria food. That particular weekend was a pleasant and relaxing one. We had the usual enjoyable chats and fine food, but then Sunday evening came, and it was time to head back to school. "Drive carefully," Mildred said as she stood in the door waving goodbye. "Oh, I'll be careful, and maybe I'll see you again in a few week," I quickly replied back to her.

Getting into the car and preparing to leave, I suddenly stopped my actions in midstream, becoming perfectly still and quiet. Before starting the car, I noticed an apparition of light in the car with me on the passenger side. The spirit was not coming through in a real definite manner, but it was still possible to see that it was a female. She had a beautiful glow around her, making it totally obvious to me that she was in spirit form, having come from the spiritual side of The Light. I did sense through Clair cognizance, or clear knowing, that she had come through from The Other Side.

She was standing, not sitting, on the front passenger side of the car interior. How is it possible for a spirit to stand in a car when that is not possible in a fifth sense way? Physically it was impossible to stand with the limited ceiling height of the car interior, but the paranormal world is free of the physical limitations we have here on Earth. Being free of both time and space, it appeared that

I was viewing her from her own dimension, and she had merely superimposed herself from her dimension into mine.

Appearing like a full grown woman, the glow from her body gave off a very comforting and effervescent light. All the colors of the rainbow were soothingly being displayed around her. Just like with other people from The Light, it was difficult to see what she was wearing because the emphasis of her being was the wonderful light that radiated from her body. It was an amazing sight to witness, and I would soon find out that she had come for a specific reason.

Spirit will very often convey a message through telepathy and thought impression. That is the way they speak with each other and often communicate to us, because in the psychic world, thoughts are things. Since there is no need to verbalize with the mouth, they merely have to think of something and transfer that thought directly to their recipient. There are times I will actually hear a clairaudient message directly into my ear, just as if they were speaking out loud to me. Yet most of the time, the normal method of conversing is through mental telepathy and thought impression.

The female that evening spoke with telepathy as I listened to her thoughts. She said, "There will be a car accident on the way back to school tonight. Keep a long distance behind the other cars." While speaking she also gave a mental impression, and I could "see" myself in my mind's eye staying far from any cars in front of me. The telepathic and clairvoyant warning had come through quite strong. After the message was given, she was instantly gone. Once again the interior of the car returned to its normal self, but the physical fifth sense interior of the car seemed quite dull and drab after witnessing a person in spirit emanating such beautiful light.

When a forewarning like this is given, I will always take it very seriously. The people on The Other Side live in a world with no past, present, or future, where time is simply measured as eternal. The fact she came to give this message meant she was able to foresee the danger approaching in my life and desired to give the warning. She was acting as a wonderful guardian and protector, wanting to keep me from potential harm.

Needless to say, I stayed extremely cautious on the way back to school that evening. The start of the trip was uneventful and normal, staying ever vigilant looking for signs of trouble, always keeping a good distance in back of the vehicles in front of me. The minutes of the journey started to add up with no signs of road danger anywhere. At first five minutes, and then ten minutes passed as I drove back toward school. Had I been imagining the visitation by spirit? That question went through my mind a couple of times.

Sometimes that is a normal reaction after some sixth sense experiences. Each experience can come through in a varying degree of intensity from the proverbial clap of thunder, to something so gentle and quiet that it is barely noticeable. This experience came through moderately strong, and yet there can still be some twinge of doubt that it ever occurred. The guardian was coming through from the spiritual side of life, so she wasn't coming through in the same dense way we view the physical world. With the higher spiritual realms being much less dense and having a much higher vibration, there are occasional times a person can feel some confusion over what they have experienced and can even question the reality of that particular event.

About twelve or fifteen minutes into the journey back to school, I was quickly becoming somewhat complacent looking for signs of road danger. In fact, the alertness in watching for trouble was fast leaving, as I had pretty much given up looking for any problems. However, I still did as the female in spirit had requested, staying a long distance in back of the vehicles in front of me. Although the traffic that evening was a little heavy on the freeways being traveled, it was still thin enough to be moving at a pretty fast speed.

After this length of time into the journey, an approaching

connector ramp was directly ahead, as one freeway connected and merged with another. As I quickly sped onto the connector, all the vehicles in the connector lanes were about to merge onto the new freeway. As we merged, something very sudden and unexpected developed. With the two freeway systems merging into one, the car in front of me abruptly started to swerve out of control. It all happened so fast, but the problem was being caused by the merging traffic. Apparently another car in a merging lane either hit or came very close to the car in front of me. This startled the driver, with that person then trying to get out of the way of the other car, quickly swaying and veering in the same lane I was in.

However it came about, there was now a car in my path spinning wildly out of control. In fact, it was not just any car, but the very car directly in front of me. Had I been keeping a close distance to this car, I would also have been involved in that developing accident. As my car whizzed through the danger area, it did look like those two cars had hit each other, and it was developing into a serious accident.

The words of the female in spirit had come prophetically true. "There will be a car accident on the way back to school tonight. Keep a long distance behind the other cars." It is amazing how spirit can not only foresee the future, but they also care so much about us, they want to guide and protect us if at all possible. I use the words "if at all possible," because I do believe there are times when spirit must retreat and let destinies take their course.

It is my belief that each of us writes our life chart before coming back to this plane of existence. A life chart is a specific guideline for our earth life, although it does have a certain amount of flexibility. Sometimes things are written into these charts which must be fulfilled and spiritual code of ethics require that spirit retreat, letting the person's life happen in the way it was intended when written. What a blessing that female from The Light appeared before the car trip. Her help and guidance proved invaluable, and without her help, the outcome for me would have been so much different that evening going back to school.

Many years later, I was no longer living in the Los Angeles area and had settled back up in Northern California. One day going out to the mailbox, I noticed a package from Mildred in the San Fernando Valley. This was the same aunt I had stayed with the weekend the warning from spirit had come through. It was a medium sized package, and right away my curiosity arose to see what she might have sent.

After opening up the brown wrapping, I found a delightful large photo of her in a beautiful frame. She was alone in the photo, since her husband had already passed a number of years earlier. It was a charming photo of her, and she was in her eighties at the time. As I looked at the photo thinking of the many nice memories of our weekend visits numerous years earlier, her spirit spoke to me through thought impression. The words came into my mind while looking at the photo, and I knew it was an important message.

How was it possible to know it was her spirit speaking? It was through Clair cognizance and clairsentience, the sixth sense abilities of clear knowing and clear feeling, where we just "know" and "feel" without any doubt. Through these two forms of psychic perception, it becomes possible to recognize a familiar spirit by their essence, the seat of their soul.

While studying the photo she telepathically said, "I just wanted to say goodbye." When she spoke those thoughts to my mind, I immediately knew what she meant. Her passing was ahead of her, and her spirit was very aware of that fact. Although her conscious mind might not have been aware of the upcoming passing; her soul knew what was ahead. Normally when a spirit begins to speak about their passing, it will happen in the distant future. It might take six months, one year, eighteen months or even longer for the event to unfold. The important thing to remember when given this type of message is that it is in the person's future, and that it will come to pass because it has been planned that way.

About one year after receiving that wonderful photo of her, one night she suddenly died in her sleep. Although she was older, there were no major health problems before her passing. Without any warning, she did have a heart attack during sleep and was quickly gone from her physical body. She had gone back to the higher realms of light, to Heaven, to be reunited with her loved ones and kindred spirits.

A number of years after she had passed, her sister also died. This sister was my other aunt that had lived in the San Fernando Valley. Lyn was an amazing aunt, always having so much love and caring in her heart for others. Her husband Joe had also previously passed years earlier. Months before she crossed over, I was shown two separate times during sleep of her passing. Both times I saw and felt Mildred planning a trip to the earth plane, ready to take her sister home to Heaven when that time came. This would make sense since they had been very close to each other here on Earth, and that eternal love bond continued despite the fact Mildred had passed years before Lyn.

Within numerous months after being shown of her passing, Lyn did leave the earth plane, going back home to God's wonderful kingdom. I spoke with a relative on the phone that gave the news of what had happened. The relative told me that the nursing home attendant said the day before Lyn passed; she kept staring at a fixed location in her room. This is often typical of many people right before they leave Earth. They will become increasingly aware of The Other Side and can actually see someone that is waiting for them to take them home. The spiritual side is opening up to them, and they are witnessing sixth sense perception. It is my true belief that Mildred was in the room that day with her sister Lyn, anxiously waiting to take her beloved sister home to The Other Side after her last heartbeat.

6

A Wonderful Beach Experience

It is my firm belief that first and foremost, here on Earth we are all spiritual beings that happen to inhabit a physical body. Through countless paranormal events during my life, I can only conclude that our spiritual side is our natural and original state of existence. We have come from that state of existence, and we will go back to that true state when we leave this Earth. Our physical and spiritual selves are very interconnected and interrelated, yet it is almost like one part of us is the real part, while the other part is like looking at our self in the mirror. The spiritual side is the more real side of the two as our senses, awareness, and reality are so much stronger on that side.

I always like to compare our physical and spiritual sides in a certain way. On this side of life, we are a body having a spirit, while on The Other Side; we are a spirit having a body. Here on Earth our physical body is dominant, while on The Other Side our spirit is dominant. Regardless of where we are, on this side or that side of existence, we are still very much ourselves. The only thing that changes between the two sides is our level of vibration due to the energy levels around us.

Since we are a body having a spirit here on Earth, it is also possible for our spirit to temporarily leave our physical body. We can often do this during sleep, always staying attached to the physical self by a thin cord known as the silver cord. It acts as a type of umbilical cord, always keeping our physical and spiritual selves joined together until it is time for us to leave this Earth. When that time comes, the silver cord will break, freeing our spiritual self from the physical body.

During our stay here on the earth plane, it is possible for our spirit to travel to other places. This is known as astral traveling, and we can travel in this manner to places right here on Earth, to the astral plane, and even to other dimensions. We are multidimensional beings and are capable of doing these things. However, our limited conscious mind will very often not remember the spiritual traveling we do.

The earth plane is very dense and has a much lower and slower vibration than the higher realms of The Other Side. This slower vibration creates some negative energy along with the existing positive energies. However, the energies here are not so low that only negativity exists. Rather, the energies on Earth are a combination of both positive and negative. There is much goodness and pureness here on Earth, but there is also negativity that is ever-present. We do have both here and from my experiences as a psychic, I do feel Earth is our classroom. It is a place to come to, experiencing both positivity and negativity, and while experiencing both, hopefully face and then overcome negative situations during our lives.

We have all had good moments during our lives, but there have also been some very hard and difficult instances. How we confront, cope with, and hopefully resolve our challenging moments here on Earth, is what makes this plane of existence such an excellent classroom. I do believe the overall progression of life is upward. Earth is giving each of us that excellent opportunity to try and do just that, to progress forward for the further development of our soul.

Sometimes it seems there is one challenge after another in our life, but we must constantly strive to achieve this goal of overcoming the negative situations we confront. Although extremely difficult at times, tapping into the higher spiritual energies can greatly help. Those energies include goodness, kindness, and unconditional caring. If we are able to tune into some of these energies and replace the negativity with positive feelings, it will greatly advance our overall growth. This is what we are here to try and do while going about our daily lives. There is a deep purpose to life here. We do have to eat, have shelter, and do all the usual activities that life involves. But we are also given the opportunity during our time here to progress and advance spiritually.

The interconnection between our individual physical and spiritual sides is very strong. However, there is also the potentially strong connection between our physical and spiritual selves with the high energies of light on The Other Side. It is possible to have those very high energies shine directly through to our physical and spiritual being. That very thing happened to me back in college.

While still attending school in Southern California, an extremely fascinating paranormal event occurred that took place on the sands of Newport Beach in Orange County. One of my favorite pastimes was to occasionally get away from school for a few hours and head to the beach. Normally, I would choose Newport Beach as it seemed to be the easiest beach community to get to, having the shortest driving distance and most direct route from school. It was always a fun excursion, and there was a great feeling of liberation and freedom getting away from the campus for a brief time. Once at the beach, it was captivating to stand on the sand and look to the horizon of the seemingly endless expanse of water.

"How would you like to go to Newport Beach with me?" I asked a fellow student and friend. "Sure, let's go. I'm through with my classes for the day," she quickly replied with an excited tone to her voice. So off we went driving down the road leaving the academic world behind, feeling a light carefree attitude and fully preparing for two hours of adventurous enjoyment. While driving down the freeway, we talked about the beach and how great it would be when we arrived there, as we kept time to some good music playing in the car. Clearly there was an anxious excitement to our mood.

After the drive to Newport Beach, we pulled into the usual parking area. From other previous trips to this location, I had already found a good lot to park in. It was good sized, and there was always an empty stall available. "There's a space right over there by the sand. Let's park there," I eagerly told my friend. Parking the car and bounding out, we were filled with a type of cheerful enthusiasm so often found in young people when taking an adventure.

"Let's go on the pier," as I motioned and pointed to the pier jutting out from the water's edge. Walking out on the wooden pier was fantastic with the smell of salt air, the crashing of powerful waves, and the blue afternoon sky. Life seemed very good at the moment, with a feeling of what more could a person ask for. Standing at the end of the pier, we looked down at the churning water. It was swirling around the pier and looked a bit inviting, but it also looked quite dangerous. I kept wondering how deep it was at that spot and if there were any undercurrents and undertows around. We continued to watch the swirling water for awhile, gazing our eyes on it almost as if in a trance.

Finally we decided to get off the pier and go walk on the sand by the water. "I just love the smell of the air here," I told my friend while filling my lungs with the fresh salty air. "Yes, it's really fresh," she excitedly replied. There we were, standing at the western edge of the North American continent with nothing but thousands of miles of Pacific Ocean in front of us. As we stood side by side, I suddenly felt a strong urge to break away from my friend and go stand closer to the water's edge by myself. As I walked closer to the water, I left her standing directly behind me. The urge to move toward the water was a powerful force, and it felt like something that needed to be done.

Standing very close to the advancing and receding water, I gazed my eyes out on the horizon. It was such a beautiful picture perfect day, with the air temperature in the higher sixties and a pleasant moderate wind blowing in off the ocean. Suddenly without warning, there was a strong inner desire to commune with spirit, and it was the White Light of the Holy Spirit I kept thinking about in my mind. There was a deep aspiration and yearning within me to direct my energies toward the higher realms and make a connection with that brilliant white light.

In order to try and connect, I maintained a straight but comfortable standing posture, arms down in front of me, with both hands in an unfolded position slightly touching each other. Next I gazed my eyes over the water, looking to the horizon, trying very hard to totally relax my mind and forget every worldly care and concern. As I did this, an amazing feeling of great peace and perfect harmony started to envelope around me. The force was commanding but at the same time perfectly gentle. It felt like the influential yet peaceful energy was coming from a dimension beyond Earth, descending from those high realms to my physical and spiritual being. In a few moments, all cares and concerns of the world had vanished and no longer mattered. In fact, it felt like they no longer existed. Standing there motionless, it seemed I had gone into an altered state of consciousness.

While this was happening, I could definitely feel the connection that had been made with the higher realms. At the time I continued to think of The White Light of the Holy Spirit, knowing through Clair cognizance it was coming from that source. During this paranormal event, my friend was being perfectly silent, and I heard no sounds coming from her.

Although I was slightly aware of activities around me, my thoughts were concentrated on the energies that were coming down from above, and the connection that had been made. Those incredible energies were sending feelings of total peace and perfect harmony. In fact at the time, it felt like the energies from this light were so strong around me, that I might even look physically different. Through clairsentience and clairvoyance, I could "sense" and "see" myself with these high vibrating energies that had been placed not only around, but also within me.

This blissful altered state continued for only a short while, possibly a few minutes at the most. It is hard to say exactly how long it lasted, but I knew if this altered state continued too long, my friend would become quite restless and nervous about what was taking place. It was a clairsentient feeling I was receiving from her, as I could feel her emotions and increasing nervousness. Because of her growing feeling of agitation, I quickly brought my state of consciousness back to the earth plane, back to Newport Beach and Earth's energies. I wanted so much to stay in that altered state and feel those incredible vibrations of white light for a while longer, but I did feel it was best to return.

After turning around and starting to walk toward her, I got to where she was standing, and then we both started to head in the direction of the car. For some unexplained reason, it suddenly felt like it was time to get back to school. While walking back to the car, she was mysteriously silent, saying nothing. After getting back inside, she kept looking at me, but once again stayed curiously quiet. The only expression she showed was a very odd look of puzzlement and confusion on her face. As we started the trip back to school, she tried to speak, but every time she started, the words just wouldn't come out. The only sound she would repeatedly make was a loud "ahh" gasping sound, which happened over and over whenever she tried to talk. In addition, her facial expression had changed from one of puzzlement to bewilderment.

Finally about fifteen minutes on the drive back to school, she finally managed to speak. She said that when I was standing close to the water's edge in front of her, that I had actually become partly transparent. She never did explain it much, only that I was "different" and instead of having a normal physical appearance, I had this unusual transparency to my body. After my friend expressed what was on her mind, she seemed to slowly calm down and finally regain her composure.

The remainder of the drive back to school was uneventful. We listened to our favorite music and after arriving back on the campus, we never again discussed what had happened on the beach that day. Why did we never again talk about that most amazing occurrence? I'm not sure I have the answer to that, although it was possibly due to the fact we were both busy with an academic and social life, and we just moved on, making the decision to never again talk about it.

What did happen on the beach that day? Looking back on it, I feel the location had a lot to do with making the experience possible. It was a beautiful setting, very calming and tranquil looking out on the blue sky and wide expanse of water. The late afternoon sun was shining down, making the water glisten and stand out like a million sparkling diamonds. All of these features helped to set the mood that day.

I did have the sudden deep desire at the time to communicate with The White Light of the Holy Spirit, and intention very often plays an important part of the sixth sense process. When we feel a deep meaningful desire within us to connect with the high realms, it helps to push the process along. Without desire and intent, it can make it much more difficult for the event to come about.

Another quality is that we must concentrate on pureness of heart and mind when reaching out to those realms. Since the energies of the higher realms are perfect in every way, we must place our thoughts on goodness and kindness. I did just that, trying to think of all things good and pure as I mentally reached out to that high vibration. When the connection was made, the powerful energy of white light enveloped my physical and spiritual bodies, raising my vibration level and allowing the high energy transparency of spirit to shine through.

It does seem totally amazing and even impossible that this could happen. However, if the connection is strong enough, it is possible. The earth plane and the higher realms are interconnected in many ways, with the two so close to each other, the separation can be thought of as a very thin veil. I feel very humbly thankful and appreciative that I was allowed to have that occurrence on the beach that afternoon. For several brief minutes, I was allowed to experience a tiny portion of the magnificent white light. It was a very special event, and the remembrance of that unusual day will always stay with me.

7

Nighttime Astral Trip

Another fascinating occurrence happened while still going to school in Southern California. I met and had become friends with another female student, and we would often sit discussing numerous topics like college students often do. The discussions would vary widely, and we would always find many things to converse about.

This young lady was from Puerto Rico and was going to school thousands of miles away from home. She had an interesting quality about her of often finding something to smile and laugh about. Her laughter was very soft and even quiet, and it would gently come out at any time during our conversations.

On one particular night, I went off to bed in my dorm room and after lying for a short while thinking of the day's activities, I drifted off into a restful sleep. It felt so relaxing and tranquil to be in that deep slumber, letting the built up academic stresses of the previous day melt away.

Dreaming during sleep is a very normal part of our lives. Some people can easily remember their dreams, while others have a hard time remembering them and might even say they never dream. From my experience as an intuitive and psychic, I have noticed our spiritual side can leave our physical body when we dream, and we can go to a place known as the astral plane. This is a plane of existence that has many levels and frequencies, which go from lower to higher. I like to think of the astral plane as the information and communication plane, a place where we can meet up with people, receive important information, or work on everyday problems of our daily lives. When we astral travel to this plane of existence, our spiritual side, also known as astral side, always remains connected to our physical body by the silver cord.

Just like in the higher realms, the astral plane has no time as we know it, and it exists without a past, present, or future. Similar to The Other Side, the astral levels are free of the physical limitations of time and space. Because there is no earthly time in existence there, we can be shown information regarding any time period.

Although we can travel to the astral plane during sleep, we can also astral travel to places right here on Earth and even go to other dimensions as well. Since we are multidimensional, our spiritual side is capable of a wide range of dimensional travel. Intent once again plays a major factor in our spirit's desire. If we truly have the desire, it does seem our spiritual side is unlimited as to where it can go, provided it is allowed by spiritual code of ethics, a code that governs spiritual law. Very often our conscious memory will not remember having traveled in this way, which is normal since many times our limited physical mind will want to try and stay in control, not wanting to explore the deeper aspects of our spiritual side.

During a deep sleep that one particular night in school, I suddenly found my spiritual astral self inside a large fancy car. Observing the interior with my spiritual eyes, it looked like it was the inside of a limousine, appearing very roomy and luxurious. Through clairsentience, or clear feeling, the interior also felt very large and spacious, with a feeling of elegance throughout. As an intuitive, feeling and knowing will usually play a very important part of many experiences. I can normally tell through clairsentience and Clair cognizance much about the paranormal event being experienced. Our spiritual side has a much greater depth of awareness than our physical side. Because of that fact, it is actually possible to sense a great deal of the situation and surroundings literally by experiencing sixth sense awareness. When in spiritual form, we just seem to sense and know much more than is possible with our conscious mind here on the fifth sense earth plane.

The air temperature inside the car felt very comfortable, and I could actually feel the cool air blowing on my spiritual body. With the windows up, it was obvious that the air conditioning was on. I knew through Clair cognizance we were in a tropical or semitropical climate and when glancing around the large interior of the car, I noticed a man sitting in the rear passenger seat. This man appeared a bit older, maybe in his late forties or even fifties, and I received the impression he was most likely monetarily wealthy, having a certain look and feel of material affluence about him.

As he sat in the soft luxurious seat, he remained perfectly silent. Obviously there was a driver, but he never spoke to the driver, and I never saw who was doing the driving. Although I was sitting fairly close to him in the car, my actual position inside the limousine seemed to be unimportant. What was important were the feelings and senses being received from the experience.

Glancing out the car windows, I noticed we were moving moderately fast with the scenery flashing by my eyes, appearing to be on a rather windy and narrow country road. It was not a high mountain road, but rather a roadway you might find in hilly terrain. Again, I sensed a tropical feel to the place, and the trees and vegetation seemed to display that feeling. There were beautiful shades of dense and lush greenery outside the window as we quickly sped along the narrow road. At one point, I could actually see through the roof of the car with my spiritual eyes, which is possible since

I was free of the physical limitations of the physical side. While looking through the roof, the verdant growth on the trees formed a wonderful moving canopy over our heads. It was exciting to be in that car, totally enjoying the experience and taking great pleasure in the moment.

Suddenly the occurrence of being inside the auto had passed. It's almost as if instantly there was a lapse of consciousness coming from my spirit. For some reason, it had been important to be inside that moving car and to have experienced it, but once it had been experienced, it was time to move on to the next astral event.

With my physical body still in a deep restful sleep back at school, I suddenly found my astral body inside a church. Just like inside the moving car, the church was also very physically real. I could tell through sense awareness this was an actual church on the earth plane. It was a specific location, and I simply wanted to enjoy the moment of being in that wonderful place of worship. The feeling inside the building was a very nice one, sensing great warmth and kindness coming from the people in attendance. Immediately, I felt the joy and cheerfulness of the energies within that church.

The people in that place of worship joyously sang, and as they did, an outpouring of love and happiness radiated from their hearts. It was truly wonderful to feel that, sensing the pure intentions and brightness that came from each of them. As they participated in the festive church service, I stood by as a silent invisible observer, watching their actions and feeling their hearts.

When the singing and service was over with, there was a great mood of camaraderie. People hugged each other and every person there had a warm glowing smile on their face. The happiness they felt in their hearts created a wonderful uplifting energy in the building, and their worshipping together brought great pleasure to everyone in the group. During this time, I continued to be the unseen observer, always watching them but never being noticed by anyone. Although I was invisible to them, my heart was not unseen and quiet. It had merged with the hearts of those in the church and the happiness everyone was feeling.

Was it possible that the wealthy gentleman in the limousine was also attending that church service? Yes, that does seem very logical and most likely probable. There was no remembrance of seeing him among the small crowd of people, but his being there would have fit in with the sequence of events that occurred during sleep that night.

Just like the experience of having traveled in the luxurious car, suddenly the church occurrence was also gone. I was no longer with those warmhearted loving people, but instead found my spiritual self back inside the limousine. However, this time was different than the first experience inside the car, and my awareness of being there was not as strong. Making this second journey inside the large vehicle did not stir my senses like the first journey had. Being inside the moving car with the outside greenery quickly passing by seemed irrelevant at this time, because what was about to happen next was of much more importance.

The third important episode during sleep that night involved visiting a large manor home tucked away in the lush tropical growth of the rolling hills. The limousine pulled up to this large home, and I got out. This home was most likely the residence of the gentleman in the car, although I am not certain of that fact. I did not remember much about the exterior façade, but rather it was the interior of the residence that carried more significance. Something was drawing my spiritual self to the inside of the home, but what was it that kept pulling at me? In a few minutes, I would discover the answer to that question.

Finding myself inside, I looked around, discovering I was in a very large room which looked and felt like a beautiful living room or central great room. The room was immense and appeared to be filled with many fine and expensive furnishings. Off in the distance was another large room, and I suddenly felt the need to take a closer look inside that area. A force kept pulling me toward that room, and I needed to see who or what that energy was.

Walking toward the room, I noticed a very long table which looked like a large dining table. As I got closer, I observed a young man possibly in his twenties sitting at the end of table. He might have been eating at the time, but my awareness was not concerned with that. Rather, it was the young man I was concerned and troubled about. Although I could not hear his thoughts, I could read his emotions and feel his heart by watching him. He was very concerned about something, and some situation was troubling him a great deal. As he sat at this long table, my thoughts were on his upsetting anxiety. It made me feel quite sad to see him acting that way, but I was just an invisible observer and really could not help him with his unhappiness. As much as I wanted to help cheer him, it was not possible.

There are spiritual laws in place that are every bit as real as our laws here on Earth. Normally, I would channel some positive uplifting energies of light over to him and try to help in that way, but my spirit seemed to know that he needed to work out this problem situation he was feeling on his own. It is also possible that he had not asked for spiritual help, and because of that, spiritual help could not be given. For whatever reason, I merely watched him, simply being a person in spirit form walking around viewing that home and the people connected to it.

Next my soul consciousness shifted to the outside, and in an instant I found myself out in the open. The air felt tropical and the lush landscaped growth was beautiful. There were a number of men standing around chatting and laughing, and I sensed the location of these men was a little distance from the main manor house. They were on the estate, but residing in a different area of the property.

It appeared they had their own living quarters and even their own small swimming pool.

As I viewed the group of men talking, my heart suddenly grew very happy. There was great joy and contentment coming from them. Sensing they were laborers of some type, I knew they belonged on the estate and did some type of work on it. The friendship and companionship they felt for each other just overwhelmed my heart with total joy. I was so happy for them that they were experiencing so much satisfaction, and that they were getting so much contentment out of life. Although they were most likely speaking either Spanish or English, their spoken word was irrelevant to me. It didn't matter what language they spoke, because I was feeling the language of elation that was coming from their hearts.

The final episode during this astral traveling experience involved a couple in the property's main swimming pool. The pool was surrounded by lush landscaping and numerous trees, being a part of the estate. It was hard to tell how far apart the pool was from the main house because of the dense growth and vegetation surrounding the pool. However far apart it was, it did give the impression of being separate and private from the main home because of the landscaping.

A male and female were in the pool swimming and through clairsentience; I felt the male in the pool was most likely the owner of the estate. Was this the older male that had been in the limousine earlier, and the male that had most likely also attended the church service? Yes, it most likely was. However, my spiritual self was not overly concerned with that fact, but instead I was much more interested in the hearts of the people being observed. Just like the young man in the dining room and the estate laborers standing chatting, I was paying close attention to the hearts of the two in the pool. Their detailed physical appearance was not nearly as important to me as the hidden emotion that was coming from them.

Watching this couple for possibly ten minutes, I noticed they were a bit older in their forties or fifties, and he was most likely the owner of the beautiful manor home. However, within an instant, I did not feel the great happiness and contentment coming from their hearts like I did the group of men. Rather, there was a feeling of insincere romance coming from the female which was not so nice to sense. The feelings were again entirely different than the emotions of the two previous encounters on the estate. The young male was feeling very troubled and upset in his heart, while the men felt great contentment and joy. The feelings coming from the couple were different again, and while observing the woman flirting romantically, I couldn't help but feel her intentions were not pure. In fact, I was almost positive at the time she was behaving that way with an ulterior motive in her heart.

While continuing to watch this couple for awhile, I felt great emptiness within me. It had been so wonderful to feel the inspirational energies of joy coming from the hearts of the men, but now those feelings were strangely absent. From the emotional energies coming from the couple, I could tell their relationship was in some ways superficial. Their involvement seemed to be based more on game playing than true love, and after studying their actions and feeling their hearts for a little while; I decided it was time to leave. My stay and visit in this semitropical land had been a very exciting and fun time. The ride in the car and the warmhearted church people, the troubled young man but joyous farm workers, and finally the romantic couple in the pool had been fascinating, but it was now time to part.

After deciding it was time to leave, something totally astounding happened. I am not sure why it happened that way, but I'm positive there was some spiritual reason for it. Turning around and starting to walk away from the couple in the pool, I started to hear my own footsteps. First one step could be heard and then the other. When this happened it rather startled me. I had been a silent observer the entire time enjoying every moment in this semitropical land, but now I was starting to physically manifest. How could this be and why was it happening? My astral body had been having a great time traveling to this place as my physical self slept at school in Southern California, but now for some reason my spiritual self was taking on some degree of physical form.

After hearing five or six of my own footsteps on the ground, I suddenly heard the female in the pool let out an astonished scream, and it was instantly obvious that she had seen me. I could sense her feelings of great surprise and bewilderment. It was not my intention to surprise and startle anyone, but for some reason I did start to take on some degree of physical form that could be seen with her physical eyes. It could have had something to do with the insincerity within her heart, and to alert her to the fact she was being observed with that type of deception. Although I have no idea what degree of physical manifestation occurred, she was able to view me in some way.

When hearing her sudden scream, I took another step or two and was gone from that estate in an instant. Wanting to leave very fast after hearing her vocal astonishment and certainly not wanting to surprise her any longer, I awoke to a pleasant Sunday morning in Southern California.

When meeting with my school friend from Puerto Rico, we briefly discussed the experience. After describing the beautiful vegetation, windy roads, and warmhearted church people to her, she quickly said, "You are describing the hill country of Puerto Rico." Then she said, "The churches are like that there. Everyone is very warmhearted, hugging each other and chatting with one another after the service." Although I mentioned the countryside and church to her, I never discussed the astral experience of the limousine and the people residing on the manor estate.

It is my belief that the friendship I had with this young lady from Puerto Rico allowed me to create a connection with her homeland. It was through knowing her and making that connection with her, that I was able to travel in spirit during sleep to her beautiful Puerto Rico.

These are two examples of the interrelationship and interconnectedness the physical and spiritual sides have with each other. In the previous segment during that sunny afternoon on a California beach, the spiritual energy of the White Light of the Holy Spirit partially manifested through my physical body, with a friend witnessing a certain degree of my body transparency. I was in physical form and yet the light of spirit from the high realms came through. While during the astral travel trip to Puerto Rico, the opposite happened with my spiritual body partially manifesting and taking on some degree of physical form. We do live in an interesting world of both physical and spiritual energies, and while on Earth, there is always a certain degree of constant connection between the two in our lives.

8

Precognitive Event

Life after college was the start of another chapter in my life. The fun days of school were now over with, and it was time to start buckling down for life and work in the real world. After graduation was over with, I headed back to the San Francisco Bay Area, full of enthusiasm and excitement like only a young person can have. That area had been my home for much of my life before going to school in Southern California, and I was eagerly returning to the area that I loved.

However, after getting settled back in Northern California, a part of me was still missing the college days down south. Southern California had become my way of life during those school years, and I continued to think of the good friends and the various activities of college life. Although it was an adjustment getting used to this new chapter of life, it was something that was necessary and was of course time to embark on. Even though it was time to begin this new phase, I still thought of those memorable college days that were in the recent past that had been a big part of my life.

Many young people know exactly what they want to do for their working career, but I wasn't one of them. Having majored in business administration, I thought at the time a career in business would be just the right type of work, and that it was the best possible choice of careers. However, after school was over with, I felt the creative arts side within me also trying to express itself. In addition to that, there was the sense awareness situation, where I very often saw, heard, and sensed things that other people weren't aware of.

These different aspects within me made a rather conflicting and confusing combination. Although I was very happy getting the business schooling and starting to work in business, at the same time it felt like something within me wanted more than just a business career. Also during this time of getting resettled back in Northern California, there was the occasional desire to visit Southern California and the surroundings that had been so much a part of my educational life.

I started working in the family business, learning various aspects of the business from the ground up. This was a good place to start learning and getting hands-on experience, since it was important to know every working part of that operation. But my heart was not exclusively satisfied with that job, and I felt a need to try something in addition to that work. For a while acting had been on the back of my mind as a fun and exciting thing to try. However, here I was with business training and starting to learn the working function of a business, which was far different from acting.

After putting some thought into it, I decided to break away from an exclusive business routine and take some modeling classes in the evening. Various research on the subject pointed out that many times it was advantageous to study modeling, get some work training in that area, and eventually use the modeling background to break into acting. The idea of trying this out seemed to satisfy an inner urge to do something in addition to simply business work. I could work with business during the day, take some modeling classes in the evening and see what developed from there. Although it felt challenging, it also sounded pleasurable as my youthful enthusiasm and excitement rapidly grew.

San Francisco at the time had a well known modeling agency. In fact, some well known people had actually gotten their acting start through this agency. They would start with a modeling career and eventually go into acting. I was in the same class with one of these well known actors that did eventually do just that. He created a modeling career and then used that career as a stepping stone into the acting world. I was now feeling pleased at giving this idea a try, and it felt like I had possibly found another calling within me in addition to business. If hard work along with some luck might smile on me, something might actually happen with the idea.

Lacking a few inches of height that is normally needed for modeling, I was pleasantly surprised after the training and ramp test, when the agency owner said I could fit into all three modeling types of high fashion, low fashion, and character. When hearing his opinion, I became ecstatic and felt the possibilities of developing work in this career might actually happen. The daytime job of working with business continued, as I contemplated how to initiate some modeling work.

As overjoyed as I was about this potential new avenue of work, there was something inside of me that didn't feel quite right, but I tried to block it out as if the feeling didn't exist. There was the desire to venture into a more creative type of work, and it was very exciting to think of this new opportunity. However, it still felt as if something was pulling me in two different directions. I very much wanted to at least try the modeling out and see what developed. But that calling within me was also being met with some type of opposition, and I could definitely sense it. What was this feeling of opposition to modeling and acting, and why was it there? Why was my intuition telling me this line of work might not be the best suited for me, despite my desire to give it a try?

At the time, some friends in Southern California wanted to give me a personal astrological chart for my birthday. They said, "We are going to an astrologer. Give us your birth date and birthplace. He will make up your chart and that will be our birthday present to you." I told them that would be great, thanking them for the very thoughtful gift. The astrologer they chose was on the teacher's staff of Carroll Righter, the King of Astrology of Hollywood. He was very well trained and was supposed to be an excellent astrologer, being well versed in that field.

Never having had much interest in astrology, my knowledge of the subject was quite limited. Occasionally reading the daily horoscope was pretty much the extent of my astrological understanding. These friends gave him my name, birth date, and birthplace. From those three pieces of information, he developed a personalized detailed chart. After they set up a time to meet with him for the discussion, the astrological chart with some notes would be explained to them and then sent up to Northern California for me to view.

The astrologer had asked that a short list of questions be prepared for him, and he would answer these questions when looking at the details of the chart. My list was rather short, but the questions asked were very vital at the time. The first and most important question was of course the potential modeling or acting career. Could one of these careers possibly work out despite the answer of "no" my instincts were telling me? Would the astrological chart have favorable answers to these questions?

The envelope containing the chart and notes of the astrology session finally arrived in the mail. With great excitement, I hurriedly tore open the envelope, having a nervous feeling of anticipation to hear what he had to say. He started by saying that I am a fire sign double Leo, and that I do thrive on movement and travel. That part seemed to be true as I had always enjoyed numerous activities and going places. Then he said something that totally surprised me.

He talked about the fact that I would be very good as an actor, but would not be happy with a modeling career. Regarding acting, he said there was no doubt about it, that I could make a career out of that profession and would do very well in it. He explained that the chart showed there was good dramatic ability, and an acting career would be well suited for me.

This was exciting to hear, however the news about modeling was rather disappointing. Even though his answer on modeling was unfavorable, his opinion on acting kept me elated as I read the notes. His comment on modeling seemed to confirm what I had felt in my heart; that it would be a fun and exciting thing to do, but it might not work out.

While continuing to read his notes, he repeatedly brought up a certain point that was discovered when studying the chart. He said that although there was no question about having good ability as an actor, my actual calling in this life was to be there for family. He said this several times in the notes, explaining there was family responsibility, and because of that responsibility, it would be very difficult to get into acting. The chart explained there was a mission in life to be there for them, and although I had free will, he thought I would take on the responsibility of what was requested of me during this lifetime.

Although I was again surprised in what he had mentioned in the notes, I didn't want to put full faith in an astrological chart. However, his words did seem to hit my heart with truth. Could this explain the pulling of different directions within me? Part of me wanted to stay in business, while another part wanted to give modeling and acting a try, which my instincts said would most likely not happen.

It has always been my belief that each of us writes a personalized life chart before coming to the earth plane. This chart is not written in stone, but rather it is a guideline for our life here on Earth. The purpose of this chart is to help guide us with goals we would like to achieve during our lifetime. These goals are very different than our earthly material goals, as they are concerned with our soul growth, the seat of our spirit. I feel when we come to Earth, it is our soul's desire to try and accomplish as many of these objectives as possible. However, since we have free will and can do whatever we want, it is possible to get off the path of our life chart. If possible, it is always best that we try and stay on the path of this all important chart, so we can expand and increase the growth of our soul, accomplishing spiritual things we set out to do before coming here.

Soul growth objectives are very different than earthly objectives. Of course while we are here, each of us needs food, some type of shelter, and other material things to support our physical life. But the spiritual world has little concern for material things. Rather, it is concerned about the growth of our true essence, which is our soul. When the day comes that it is time to leave this Earth, it won't matter how wealthy or not wealthy we were in the material sense. What will matter will be the type of person we were while here, and what we did to make this a better place. A friendly smile that is much appreciated to a stranger feeling very depressed, or giving a helping hand to someone in need. These are the types of things our soul growth is concerned with, along with specific objectives in our life chart.

Although the astrological chart was fascinating, it was still quite disappointing. However, it did raise a very significant question within me. Is there a connection and link between our life chart written before we come here and our astrological chart based on our name, birth date, and birthplace? It certainly seemed there could be a definite connection between the two, and the astrological chart was merely stating what I had been sensing in my heart about the life chart. The fact I felt a desire to give modeling or acting a try, but also felt it might not happen, and it might not take place.

During this period of career confusion, more fascinating experiences started to occur. It was the middle of summer, and I was excited about getting away for the weekend. Friday afternoon had finally arrived, and it was time to leave town for a few days, heading up to Lake County for a nice relaxing weekend getaway. The thought of sitting by the lake and soaking up some sun rays sounded fantastic. Friday afternoon was here, and I was going to make the most of it.

The first part of the drive up to Lake County was uneventful. Listening to some music, I continued to think of how nice it would be to get to the lake. After about 1 hour into the 3 hour journey, the drive seemed perfectly normal with traffic moving moderately fast. However without any type of warning, I suddenly felt a terrible explosion to my head, and immediately after that, it appeared the road had turned upside down. The road appeared where the sky should be, with the sky down below the road.

This was extremely frightening and many thoughts suddenly surged through my mind. What is going on, why is this happening, and is there something physically wrong with me? Nothing different were happening in the physical sense, as I continued to drive normally, but this odd appearance of the road bewildered me. It was all so confusing and it had happened so fast, with one moment everything being perfectly normal and the next second feeling the very powerful explosion to the head with the road appearing to turn upside down.

Driving about fifty-five miles per hour at the time, I wondered about slowing down and trying to stop the car. Maybe that is what I should have done, but instead I continued to drive. My instinct said it would be ok and not to worry about what was happening. Although my instinct was saying one thing, my emotions were feeling quite the opposite. It was extremely alarming to be experiencing this. The road above me was just as real as if it were happening in the physical sense, and yet it wasn't happening physically. I was viewing and experiencing something that was paranormal and sixth sense. It was all so confusing and having no idea what to do, I continued to drive at that speed for possibly eight or ten seconds, constantly praying that whatever was happening would quickly leave.

After the eight or ten seconds, suddenly it was gone, leaving as fast as it had come. The road once again appeared normal and was beneath the vehicle. The head felt fine and everything once again seemed usual. After the roadway appearance returned back to normal, a huge sigh of relief came across me. What a feeling of liberation after having experienced such a terrifying ordeal. But what had just taken place and why did it occur?

Throughout my life, I had been experiencing many unusual occurrences and events. This strange incident seemed to be yet another odd experience to add to the list. My physical health was ok and there was nothing wrong in that aspect. So I continued with the journey, trying not to think too much about what had just happened. The remainder of the drive up to Lake County was fine, and that weekend was enjoyable, soaking up some sun and having some much needed relaxation time.

I never thought much more about that experience until the following year. It was then that I looked back upon the peculiar incident of that particular summer day, realizing it was an exact vision and precognitive awareness of something yet to come in the future. Precognition, the ability to foresee or experience the future through sixth sense awareness, had clearly been shown to me. The following year would reveal why that puzzling event had occurred.

Months after that psychic event; I took a trip down to Southern California to visit some friends for several days. My hoped for start in modeling was still in limbo, as I continued to feel the strong pull toward family and working in that business. Because of that strong feeling, I continued to have many mixed emotions regarding my work and career situation. However, it was time to momentarily forget about that and just have some fun getting away, visiting with friends in Southern California.

During the stay, I suddenly entertained an impulsive idea. Enjoying the area and feeling very comfortable with that location, the thought came to mind that it might be worthwhile to just stay in that area for awhile and try to find some work. Many times young people in their mid-twenties can be quite spontaneous and make spur of the moment decisions. For most, their lives are just starting out, and they very often take advantage of that fact, trying to find the exact niche in life where they feel comfortable. I was no exception to this spontaneity, and even thought work in that area might lead to an eventual acting opportunity. Although I continued to feel pulled in opposing directions, I was seriously thinking of staying in that locale for at least a time.

One day during the visit with friends, I called Dad at his office in Northern California. We had a normal short conversation, and I said nothing to him about my plan to stay in Southern California for a bit. However, toward the end of that phone chat something very unusual happened. Although he had always wanted me to do what I chose to do, he suddenly spoke three powerful words and said, "We need you."

It was totally out of character for him to say something like that. He had always wanted me to do what I desired in life, and yet now, without any warning, he suddenly spoke those three important words. When he said that, my thoughts went back to the astrology chart and what the astrologer had to say, that there was some type of responsibility within the family. Dad's words reminded me of the astrologer's message that it would be difficult to get away from what the family, on a spiritual level, had requested of me. My thoughts also went to the constant feeling within me of family duty, despite the fact I had just made a decision to stay for awhile in Southern California.

Those three words were a life changing event, and they left me feeling stopped in my tracks. When he said that, there was a tone of urgency in his voice. He was not pleading, but he did say it in such a way that I knew he was very serious and meant what he had said. At that point, it did seem the astrologer might have been correct when he said there was some type of family accountability, and it was something that was meant to be in my life.

Clairaudience is the ability to hear beyond the normal range of hearing, with many psychic and intuitive people having that ability. I have had it often throughout my life, and for me clairaudience can take on various forms. When a spirit is trying to communicate in this way, sometimes it will sound like a person is actually speaking directly into my ear, just as if they were standing next to me or even speaking to me on the phone. At other times, the voice of the spirit seems to originate more from the inner ear rather than the outer ear. And yet in other instances, the voice tends to be muffled and soft, almost like a thought going through my head, which can happen either during sleep or when awake. This type of spirit communication can come from those still alive on Earth as well as those who have passed over. We all have a spirit, and the clairaudient message can be sent from anyone, whether they are here on the earth plane or have departed.

When Dad spoke those three words "We need you," I do feel it was his spirit that I was hearing over the phone. Many times I can not tell the difference whether it is a physical or spiritual voice, since sometimes they do sound the same. I do feel it was his spirit that had sensed the potential turning point of my decision to stay in Southern California for awhile. There was a feeling within me the decision to stay there might actually turn into a relocation to that area. With his spirit being aware of what I was thinking and the fact it might actually turn into a longer stay, he needed to express what the future should hold for me. The fact I never said anything during our phone conversation about staying in Southern California for awhile, made me realize it was his spiritual side making that request of needing me.

Our spiritual soul mind is a lot more aware and has much finer senses than our physical conscious mind. In addition, there is no earth time in the spiritual world since everything is simply measured by the event and not by time. Spiritually we can know the past, present, and future, but much of the time that information is blocked from our conscious mind. On that day during our phone conversation, it was made very clear to me that whatever was ahead in my future; I was needed by family and was meant to be there for them. The following year would provide the answer to that puzzling question.

PART II

9

Before The Change

The next year was a continuation of events in this new chapter of my life following college. I do believe when each of us writes our life chart before coming here, they are written in such a way that we actually have different segments to our life. Each segment is a phase where we confront certain situations and events, hopefully coming to some type of favorable resolution. After working on that chapter's situations, it is then time to put closure to that part of our life, moving on to the next set of life's circumstances and events.

January 1st arrived. It was a brand new year, and there was the feeling of renewed hope and enthusiasm that a new year normally brings. During the first part of January, something peculiar happened. While talking with Mom and Dad, for no conscious reason and without any premeditation, I suddenly blurted out a short phrase to them that totally surprised and startled my conscious self. I quickly told them that "This is the year of the change." It amazed me how the words just flowed out of my mouth without any forethought about what was being said. There was an extremely strong urge within me to tell them that message. But why did I say that and what did it mean? They were silent after those words were spoken, and I imagine they were trying to figure out exactly what I was talking about. However, they gave no reply to that odd comment, never asking why I would say something like that.

This happened repeatedly during the first part of that year. Sometimes when talking with them, I would always repeat the same phrase that "This is the year of the change." I couldn't stop myself from frequently saying that as those words bubbling within me needed to be told. They needed to know that it was a very different year, and there would be a major change that would occur. This inner urge to tell them was so powerful; it could not be kept silent.

As the months passed, I occasionally continued to tell them this message, but they never asked what it meant, which in a way was rather odd. They were used to my sixth sense predictions and warnings, so they simply listened, with their conscious minds most likely wondering what the rambling was all about. Our conscious mind is very often in the dark by the reality of our spiritual side. Many times our consciousness can try to block out this reality and actually be successful at it. However, we are much more than mere physical beings, and Dad was about to display that fact.

In the spring of that year, Dad and I were sitting outside enjoying the warm sunshine. It was a glorious day and the warmth from the sun felt good after the cool winter rains. As we sat there, he started visiting with me, and during the chat, I noticed he had a glow around him with some beautiful colors radiating from him. Also looking back on that discussion, I had no recollection of his mouth moving as he talked.

By this time in my life, I was very used to experiencing many different types of paranormal occurrences. To be honest, there didn't seem to be anything that unusual since the physical and spiritual sides interconnect so strongly for me. He was communicating a message, and I just sat listening to him with great interest. In hindsight, the conversation seemed normal except for the glowing colors around him, and also the fact I had no remembrance of his mouth moving. During this discussion he told me that he was going to be passing. He also said that he wanted me to be there for Mom, being sure to watch over her whenever possible after he was gone. His talking continued for quite a while, although my conscious mind could not remember everything he had said. However, the important point he wished to get across was that he wanted me to be there for her after he had departed the earth plane.

Looking back upon our chat, it became obvious that his spirit had spoken to me. That understanding would explain the glow around him with the beautiful colors, as I was seeing his spiritual body shining through the physical. Our spiritual body does not have the denseness of the physical body, and having a higher energy level, it is composed of light energies rather than being physically solid. This would also explain why I had no recall of his mouth moving. In spirit there is no need to talk like we do in the physical sense, since discussion can be done through mental telepathy and thought impression.

Thinking back upon that spring day, it is apparent Dad's spirit knew his passing was imminent. Since each of us writes our individual life chart, it is possible for our spiritual side to read that chart, looking to see when our departure time is approaching. I do believe we have various exit points to choose from during our lifetime, and it was a certainty from his talk that he was going to use the upcoming exit point to make his departure from Earth.

It is fascinating that our spiritual self through our soul mind can know so much and be so aware, yet our physical side and conscious mind can very often be kept in the dark about many matters. Normally there is a great amount of spiritual knowledge that does not get through to the conscious mind. Dad's spirit knew what was going to happen, yet his conscious self most likely remained totally unaware. It is possible for the conscious mind to connect more with the soul mind, but for many people, the mind in the physical body remains unaware of many spiritual things that are taking or will take place.

That spring discussion with Dad brought many aspects of the past few years of my life together. The fact he wanted me to be there for Mom and help her after his passing, explained why I kept feeling a pulling towards family responsibility, despite the fact I was thinking of modeling or acting. It also explained why the astrologer had said acting would be difficult since there was duty within the family, and I would be expected to take on that responsibility. Regarding the phone call from Southern California up to Dad's office in the Bay Area, it was also now clear why his spirit had spoken over the phone saying, "We need you," when I was silently thinking of staying in Southern California for a time.

However, there was one connection to the puzzle that had not yet been fulfilled. In January, I had started to verbally alert them that "This is the year of the change." Could it be that his passing would happen during that year? That part of the riddle remained unfulfilled.

Despite the fact Dad and I had that conversation; I tried to put it out of my conscious mind, creating separation from what he had said. It was much too painful to remember on a conscious level, and yet it was something that had been planned and apparently would happen. Although spiritually I was very aware of what he had said, the physical side of me wanted no part of it.

Many times it can be difficult for an intuitive and psychic, since they are often aware of upcoming events that aren't always pleasant to think about. The passing of a loved one is definitely at the top of that list. None of us want to be cognizant about an unpleasant event in the future, and yet for the person using sixth sense perception, knowing of a loved one's passing ahead of time can happen. Spring turned into summer that year as I sporadically told both Mom and Dad about the upcoming change for that year. My constant message to them seemed a bit unrelenting, but it was just something inside of me that needed to come out.

As the days grew longer and warmer, I kept busy with my usual work schedule. Then on the evening of July 1st at ten thirty at night, a very unusual experience happened. I was busily preparing for bed, when suddenly without any warning; a male voice spoke softly into my ear. His message was very short and he simply said, "This is it. This is the change." The male was of course in spirit form since there was no one else physically in the room at the time. Out loud I quickly threw a statement back to him. In a tone of some denial and even unpleasantness, I immediately said, "Things don't look any different to me." At the time, I felt quite perplexed why I would instantly answer spirit in such a manner, when normally I would never answer a message in that way. But his communication stirred something deep within me, and my conscious self wanted no part in hearing what he had to say. So at ten thirty at night having received that message which greatly bothered me, I went off to bed, trying very hard to forget he had even said that.

The following morning, Dad had some out of town business to tend to. He was going to take a trip north and would be gone for a couple of days. On the morning of July 2nd, I called him at his office and said something to him that had never been said before. During our brief phone conversation, I told him to enjoy his drive north, hoping his drive would be very pleasant and relaxing. Continuing to talk without any forethought and premeditation, I suddenly said, "You are a great Dad. You rate an 'A plus' with me, and I love you." During that short phone call, an inner desire came over me to give him that message. It was something that needed to be said at that particular time.

After the brief call, we hung up and I consciously wondered why there had been such an urgency to speak those words. Of course my spiritual self already knew the reason, and it was my spiritual self wanting to give him that message. It was a farewell message letting him know he had been the greatest Dad, and he was getting a superior mark on his life's report card from one of his sons. Although my spiritual self already knew why that was said, my conscious mind questioned why, most likely because I really didn't want to make the spiritual connection and consciously know.

It was now the day after the message from the male in spirit, a message that was explicitly clear that some great change was at hand, and the time had arrived. Dad was going to be driving north from San Francisco, and he would be using the same freeway that I had used one year earlier when suddenly experiencing the feeling of an explosion to the head with the appearance of the road turning upside down. The day of July 2nd passed without incident until around 6 p.m. that evening. At that time I received a phone call from a hospital in Santa Rosa, a city north of San Francisco. Dad had been in an auto accident around three thirty that afternoon with his vehicle having a tire blowout going around a curve.

Later we found out that he had lost control of the vehicle due to the blowout, and it had spun out of control, quickly turning over upside down. In addition, the force of the accident had ejected him out of the vehicle. After the paramedics arrived, he was immediately transported to a hospital in Santa Rosa. The person on the phone told me his condition was critical, and they wanted family members to come immediately, informing me they would also contact other family members.

After the shocking news, I explained the situation to Mom, and we both went into total stress mode. When a person receives a call like that, many times there is a feeling that it isn't real, that it can't possibly be happening. That is exactly how we felt as we kept trying to tell ourselves that he would be ok and everything would be fine. Yet deep down through Clair cognizance, I knew it was much more serious than that. When tuning into the energies of the situation, it felt very ominous and impending.

We quickly got ready for the hour's drive to the hospital, and after hasty and rapid preparation; we were ready for the trip north. Hastily getting into the car, we immediately set out for Santa Rosa. During the drive north we were both strangely silent, with each of us locked into our own private thoughts. It was almost as if we were afraid to talk about it, so each of us kept our thoughts within ourselves. I kept telling myself that he would be ok, but that was my conscious mind trying to rationalize and solve the problem. My soul knew differently.

When we arrived at the hospital, we quickly gave them our name and asked where we should go. Immediately they directed us to a section of the hospital that had a good sized lobby and waiting room. One of my brothers and his wife had already arrived, but my other brother had not yet received the news. At the time, my mind was very blurred and confused, with numerous thoughts rushing through my head. Still feeling stunned, I kept wondering how this could be happening to our family. Over and over I kept trying to tell myself that he would be ok and after a short stay in the waiting room, the nurses took us into see him. The doctor spoke, telling us Dad's situation was extremely critical and grave. With all the numerous injuries from the accident, there was no way his physical body could recover.

I looked down at Dad, a man that several hours earlier had been robust and very much alive. Now he was motionless except for his eyelids. They kept quivering at a rapid pace like they were trying to open, but in hindsight it was most likely the process of his spirit preparing to leave his physical body. The doctors told us it was amazing that he was still alive, but I think he was waiting for us to come to the hospital so we could see him for the last time, and he could say goodbye to us in his own way. He wasn't able to speak, but he wanted us in the hospital when he passed.

Just as quickly as we had been ushered into see him, suddenly the nurses and doctors rushed us back out into the waiting room again. I really don't know why they did that, but it was certainly possible it was done that way for medical reasons. Mom wanted to be with him, but they insisted we go into the waiting room. We did ask if there was a chapel in the hospital, and they kindly directed us to its location.

Both Mom and I went into the chapel and sat in a pew, with the situation continuing to have a feeling of unreality. Hours earlier life had been normal, and we were all very happy going about our everyday activities. Now several hours later we suddenly found ourselves sitting in a hospital chapel, praying for a very special loved one. Feeling tired, confused, and helpless, we silently prayed asking that God would somehow heal Dad and make everything ok.

The remembrance of what the male in spirit said the previous night had totally slipped my conscious mind. I had temporarily forgotten about his message that "This is it. This is the change." I had also momentarily forgotten about having experienced the precognitive explosion to the head and the upside down roadway one year earlier. Our only concerns at the time were the thoughts and prayers being offered while sitting in the silent chapel. We prayed with all our hearts that God would somehow make him well, and that this terrible experience would have a happy ending. God did make him well and provide a happy ending, but in a way that we were not praying for. A miraculous change for Dad was about to occur, and God would bless me, allowing me to experience through paranormal awareness the incredible transformation that was about to happen.

10

The Change Arrives

After sitting in the chapel for awhile, we slowly walked back to the waiting room. Our emotions were filled with total helplessness and great sadness. We wanted so much for Dad to be ok and for everything to be as it had been six hours earlier. There was soft music playing in the waiting room coming from an overhead ceiling speaker, and although the music was nice, it did nothing to soothe our spirits. Those in our family at the hospital felt so lost at the time, it seemed like our world was caving in.

Without any warning, I suddenly noticed the music from the overhead speaker had started to sound unusual. It sounded like nothing I had ever heard before, and in an instant, it had become so much more peaceful and serene. Moments earlier the music was doing nothing to soothe my inner turmoil, yet now it seemed at once to touch my soul and raise my spirit. There was so much calm within the music, a feeling of peace and contentment that is not known in this fifth sense world. At the time, it never occurred to me that a sixth sense experience was beginning. Clairaudience, the ability to hear beyond the normal range of hearing, was commencing.

Listening to the music, it sounded like each individual note was separate and detached from the other notes. During that time a clairvoyant image occurred. Clairvoyance is the paranormal experience of seeing something in our mind's eye. Many psychics call this the mental third eye within the head located between and slightly above our two eyes. During clairvoyance, this third eye will psychically open, so we can literally see an image with our mind. It is almost like watching a slideshow, and if there is movement, like watching a movie scene. Clairvoyantly I saw the notes from the music, with each note floating very softly and gently in the air. Every note had a beautiful tone far exceeding any sound here on Earth. It was all very inexplicable, but yet so magnificent to hear and see.

Next another entrancing clairvoyance appeared. This psychic perception was of colors, beautiful multi-hues that were so brilliant and vibrant, there was certainly nothing like this on the earth plane. As I watched the colors through my mind's eye, they formed a breathtaking kaleidoscope of shining radiance. What did these experiences signify; the great feeling of peace within the music along with such beautiful colors?

After the clairaudient and clairvoyant experiences came a clairsentient feeling. Clairsentience is the art of physically or emotionally feeling beyond what is logically possible, and is yet another type of paranormal event. Along with the heavenly music and breathtakingly radiant colors came a great feeling of going home. It felt like a grand welcoming home party was about to commence, as the joy and happiness expanded far beyond Earth. The bliss was endless and the rapture was eternal.

The doctor slowly walked into the waiting room and came over to us with a very somber look on his face. He directed his words to all of us, but most specifically to Mom. He softly said, "Robert has passed." The doctor explained that Dad could no longer put up the fight with the extent of his injuries, and that he had passed quietly. They had tried to keep him comfortable, but there really was nothing the medical team could do. Yet another shock of disbelief went through all of us. Could this actually have happened and was it actually possible he was gone? As much as I hoped it was only a terrible unreality, I quickly came to my senses, realizing it did of course happen in a very real sense. In a matter of hours, our lives had been changed in a monumental way.

After some brief arrangements and paperwork, we walked back to our cars for the return trip home. What had started out as a normal day abruptly ended so differently. The male in spirit form had been totally correct when he spoke to me the night before, clearly stating, "This is it, this is the change." At the time, I was quite aloof and even defensive not wanting to hear what he had to say. However, he was amazingly accurate with his timing and the fact that less than twenty-four hours later, Dad had passed. It was indeed a huge change for everyone. I was accurate when repeatedly telling Mom and Dad throughout the year that "This is the year of the change." Dad was also right when we talked on the phone the previous year, with him in Oakland and me in Southern California. Because I seriously thought of staying in Southern California for awhile and possibly making an eventual relocation to that area, his spirit suddenly spoke over the phone to me and said, "We need you." Dad was also exact that one spring day months before his July passing, when his spirit told me that he would be passing soon, and he wanted me to be there for Mom. Lastly, the astrologer turned out to be precise when he said my astrological chart showed there was family responsibility, and that I would find the strength and courage to be there for them.

About one year earlier, I had mysteriously felt the tremendous explosion to the head with a vision of the road turning upside down. It had been just as real as if it had occurred in the physical sense, but it was instead paranormal. Amazingly, my experience happened on the same road and in the same location as his auto accident. On that same freeway approximately one year later, he did experience the explosion to the head during the accident with the vehicle then overturning. My psychic experience was truly a precognition of what was to happen the following year.

Although this was an extremely distressing time for our family, there was one exceptional bright spot shining vibrantly through all the sadness. From the paranormal events that occurred in the waiting room of the hospital, there is no doubt in my mind that I experienced his passing as it was taking place with him. He was going to a world that is so beautiful and glorious; it goes far beyond anything we have here on Earth. He was going home to The Other Side.

It is my belief that Heaven is our true home, while Earth is just a temporary place to further develop our soul growth. We come to Earth to experience the combination of positivity and negativity. With the preplanned objectives of our life chart, we can hopefully overcome negative experiences on this earth plane and reach our spiritual life objectives, further advancing our soul. We can actually advance faster on the earth plane than in the higher realms of The Other Side. Since the higher realms have no negativity, there are no negative challenges to work with. But by experiencing and hopefully prevailing over these difficult experiences on Earth, we are actually strengthening the seat of our spiritual being, which is our soul.

The beautiful music and incredible colors I experienced in the waiting room that evening as Dad was passing allowed me to witness a tiny portion of the true magnificence of that place. The strong bond between the two of us created a powerful connection, so it was possible for me to actually feel what was happening to him during his passing. I feel very confident there were many loved ones waiting to greet him as he entered that breathtaking place. The joy and unconditional love of Paradise was waiting for him, and it truly was the greatest welcoming home party, with his loved ones anxiously greeting him on his return back home.

Why did the precognition on that road trip happen the previous year? It truly was a precognitive event, but what brought it about? The concepts of time and space are entirely different in Heaven. Time always seems to be in the moment there, while space is also different, with it becoming possible to have large numbers of people in a very small space. Since there is no past, present, or future in Heaven, time is eternal. I feel the astral plane is the plane of existence between Earth and The Other Side. Because it is a spiritual plane, it also has the same concepts of time and space as Heaven.

One year before Dad's passing; the auto accident was imminent and it was going to happen on that road location. It had been written into his life chart and when spring came, his spirit spoke to me, telling me his passing was approaching. There has always been a strong bond between the two of us, and since there is no time as we know it on the astral plane, I was able to tune into that future event. His passing was already a well known fact on the astral level, and with our strong connection bound by love, my physical body immediately reacted the moment I drove over that portion of roadway. Driving over the location of his accident, I then experienced something very similar to what he experienced one year later.

Months after he had passed, I decided to take Mom out for dinner. We were going to meet up with some friends in another town and hopefully have a nice meal. It did seem like the right thing to do, and it felt like it was time to start living again. After we decided on the meal out, I suddenly received a very joyful and uplifting feeling. It was a great sensation, and it felt like we were going to have a fantastic evening. This feeling of happiness and enjoyment stayed with me as we were driving to meet our friends. I could tell the energy was coming in from the higher realms, since it had a feeling of great elevation to it. The energy also had the clairsentient feeling that everything was perfect and everything was fine. What did this happiness mean? It was obviously coming in from a very high level, but who was sending it? At the time, little did I know what a remarkable evening it would turn out to be.

We met our friends and quickly headed for the restaurant. When we got to the eatery we sat down at the table, and once again I felt energy of pure elation and happiness. It was such an inspirational feeling, and it brought much contentment to my soul. We had a delicious meal with lots of laughter and smiles. It felt like the sadness of Dad's passing had greatly lessened, and we were once again starting to enjoy life. The grief of the previous months had been replaced with jubilation and cheerfulness. It was also interesting that I was not the only one feeling this uplifting energy. All four of us at the table seemed to be experiencing it.

On the way home that evening, I kept thinking of the nice time we had at the restaurant. It felt so good to once again feel laughter in our hearts. We had just experienced many weeks of unhappiness and grief, so this evening was a great change for the better. About five miles from home, I suddenly felt an urge to look in the back seat. It was an inner urge, and a telepathic thought kept telling me to look.

While driving, it was a little difficult to turn around and glance, so instead I chose to take a look in the rear view mirror. What happened next was totally astounding; looking through the mirror I saw Dad sitting in the back seat with a contented smile on his face. Could this actually be happening that his spirit was with us in the car? Not trusting the rear view mirror, I had to see Dad with my own eyes. If the rear view mirror was playing tricks on me, I had to know for sure. For a brief couple of seconds, I quickly turned my head and looked at the back seat. Much to my delight and pleasant surprise, Dad was indeed sitting there. He looked directly at me while I looked at him and when we made eye contact, there was no doubt that he knew I had seen him.

Many people might have been very alarmed and even traumatized to see a male spirit sitting in the back seat. However, by this time of my life, I was used to the totally unexpected world of the paranormal. Seeing him came as no great upset, but rather I was very delighted and felt a great inner peace knowing that he was with us.

He looked great, and he had a real glow of everlasting joy around him, coming down from The Other Side to be with us for a brief time. From personal experiences, it is my definite belief that each person in Heaven is eternally young and in the prime of their life. However, a person in spirit can also change their appearance, much like we would put on a different set of clothing. They can show them self in different ways and can appear as old or young as they wish.

For those brief few seconds when looking at him, I noticed he appeared about the same age as he was before he died. He did appear older, since he passed over at the age of sixty-five. However, he showed himself at that age for a reason. If he had become perceptible as a youthful thirty year old like he is in Heaven, he was most likely concerned that I might not have recognized him. This could have happened, but when I see familiar spirit and communicate with them, I will normally know who it is by "their essence." Their essence is their inner soul being. It is the real "them" that makes them an individual from everyone else. If he had shown himself as a youthful thirty year old male, it is most likely I would still have known who it was by his essence. However, he wanted to be sure that I recognized him, so he appeared very much the way he had looked at his older age on Earth.

Although he became observable as an older male, I could immediately tell he was coming in from an elevated vibration level. He looked to be in his early or mid-sixties, but he had no wrinkles. His skin was smooth as silk with not one blemish or marking. This was the telltale sign that he had come in from The Other Side. With the very high energies that exist in Heaven, people do not have wrinkles. Since Heaven is an eternal place, they are also eternal looking in appearance. So although he did show himself as older, the fact he had no wrinkles proved he was definitely paying a visit from Heaven.

He was wearing his favorite set of clothes, a casual shirt with a light blue pair of pants. While on Earth, he had smoked a pipe the latter part of his life. In the back seat of the car that evening, he was once again smoking his favorite pipe. He knew that I could see him, and no doubt he was extremely happy that I could view him in spiritual form.

Suddenly a dilemma occurred to me. Should I tell Mom, who was quietly sitting on the passenger side, that her husband was in the back seat? At first it felt like a hard decision to make, but after a few moments I decided not to tell her. There was a possibility she might not be able to see him by the time I explained it to her. If his manifestation was gone by the time she looked, I didn't want her to question what I had said. It might actually have upset her if I could see him and she couldn't. She did trust me a lot, but there was still a chance she might question what I had said. For that reason after a few seconds of thought, the decision was made that it was best not to tell her.

I am not sure how long his appearance in the back seat lingered since I didn't look back again. However, I'm positive he was thrilled that I had seen him, and that he had accomplished a spiritual manifestation. He had made himself known to me, and through clairsentience, I felt he was very contented with the visual connection that had been made.

When we arrived back home, we went inside the house, and I immediately knew Dad had walked in right behind us. It was a Clair cognizant feeling of knowing, and there was no question it, he was there. A few minutes after being in the house, the phone rang and I answered. After talking on the phone for several minutes, I hung up when suddenly Dad spoke into my ear. I am not sure why it happens this way, but whenever spirit speaks in this manner, it is always my right ear they speak into and never the left. His message was short and to the point, which is normally the case with spirit communication, and he simply said, "I have to go." Clairvoyantly with my mind's eye, I saw him walk right past me and through an open door several feet away. In an instant, he was gone.

What an inspirational evening that had turned out to be. When getting ready to go out for the meal, there was a feeling of great cheerfulness and joy. In hindsight, I was sensing the fact Dad was going to be with us that evening. The feeling of contentment and elation was coming from Dad's energies and the energies of The Other Side.

When a person passes and leaves the earth plane, they will for a certain length of time, still feel the physical connection of just having lived on earth. They have only just recently made the transition from a body having a spirit to a spirit having a body, going from this dimension to The Other Side. With the earth life that has just ended, they do have the recent memory and connection of what it was like to be in physical form. For that reason, it seems easier for the spirit to show them self to the person they wish shortly after their passing. Once they become fully acclimated to their new life on The Other Side, although still possible, it seems to become a bit harder for them to manifest. However, that does not mean they aren't with us. Their love is always with us, and they do come around us. It is the connection of love that binds us with our special ones on The Other Side, a connection that will never be broken. That year a very big change arrived for our family, and a new chapter in our lives began.

11

Angels Gather

Years ago our family had a good friend that lived just down the road from us. She was a delightful person, always having the biggest smile on her face with a heart of gold to match. I'm not quite sure how we met, but over the years she had become a very close acquaintance to us.

Ruby was one of those people that never met a stranger. She would greet everyone with a warm hello, quickly making any person she was talking with feel perfectly comfortable and at ease. Ruby was just a kind hearted, down-home type of person that radiated a great amount of charm and personality.

Many times on the spur of the moment I would call her up and say, "Ruby, we are having some bar-b-qued hamburgers tonight. Would you like to come over and have dinner with us?" She would always reply with a fast response of "Oh yes, I'd love to." If she was having an out of town guest at her home, I would tell her to bring her guest as well. We had many good times together, and our conversations were always filled with smiles and enjoyment. The visits with Ruby always proved to be very uplifting and heartening.

One time she decided to go out of state to stay with relatives for a visit and planned to be gone about ten days. At the time, she lived on a couple of acres and had some pet geese. When she found out that she was going to leave and visit with family, she asked if I would feed and take of the geese for her while she was gone. "Sure, that will be no problem," was my quick reply after she had asked. Before she left on her trip, I went over to her house, and she briefly told me how to take care of them.

The afternoon came for her departure. She was very excited about the journey since she seldom got away from home, and she politely reminded me to be sure and take good care of her "babies" while she was gone. I reassured her they would be in good hands and would be well taken care of. That put a big smile on her face, and that comment seemed to end her nervousness about leaving her pet geese.

Although I had quickly offered to do this for her, it was going to be a totally new experience for me. I was basically a city boy, mostly raised in the confines of cities and suburbs. Our family had always had a dog or two, but taking care of some geese was going to be a new experience. This was something I was actually looking forward to; thinking the job of tending to them would be quite simple and easy.

Ruby lived close to a busy road with a good amount of traffic. Because of the high traffic volume and the neighborhood dogs, she had a pen house built for the geese to stay in at night. It was a small shelter, but it provided protection for the geese during nighttime hours. In the morning, she had asked that I let them out and then put them back inside the little pen house before dark. She had also explained where the food was and how often to feed them.

The day she left on her vacation, she kept them in the pen for the night. The following morning came to tend to the geese, and I dutifully went over to Ruby's home, opening up the pen house door. There were several of them, and they quickly shuffled out the opened door of the shelter, very happy to be back out in the open and once again free to roam around on her property. Their loud vocal honks filled the morning air as they hurriedly waddled away from the pen house.

Early evening came and I went back over to her house to put the geese back into the shelter. Ruby had said the way to get them back in their pen was to call out to them, yelling out "Here girls," and then leading them back to the pen once they came. So that is exactly what I did, standing close to the pen and feeling quite ridiculous calling, "Here girls." At the time, I thought it would be a very easy task, they would politely come, and I could lead them into their pen. Once they were inside, I would hurriedly put some grains in and close the door. Then they could feast on the grains in the safety of the approaching late evening and night.

However to my surprise, they didn't come. In fact, the more I tried to call them and gain their attention, the more they turned the other way and very stubbornly refused to acknowledge me. That put me into a certain degree of panic mode. With the early evening eventually turning into night, it was necessary to get them inside before dark. During that time of year, the sun would not set until quite late, but it would be coming within several hours. I kept thinking to myself "What am I going to do?"

It would have been comical to watch if anyone had been viewing the situation. I was not used to geese and especially not familiar on how to take care of them. Trying to chase after them, I had hoped to maneuver them back into their pen. But of course, that effort quickly failed since they were much faster than I was. Going back to my home with a feeling of concern and upset, I figured if they weren't going to go back into their pen on their own, there was no way I would be able to get them in there. At the time, I felt the situation was rather hopeless and without promise.

Later that evening, I went back over to her property in the hopes things might be different and there might possibly be a better outcome. By this time it was getting quite late, and the sun would soon be starting to set. Much to my surprise, a favorable turn of events was about to happen. After getting there, I found they were already standing next to the door of the pen house. So I simply opened up the pen door, and they promptly went inside without any hesitation. What a great relief that was. Quickly throwing some grains inside and checking their water; I rapidly closed the door of the pen house. With night fast approaching, they were now back in their home safe and free from potential nighttime danger.

Animals are very smart and many times much smarter than we even realize. They knew I was a stranger to them and for that reason; they would not come to me like they would for Ruby. However, when night started to quickly approach, they were more than happy to go into the safety and security of their little house. Before Ruby left on vacation, she had requested that I feed them a certain amount. Despite the exact amount she mentioned, I was feeling a bit generous with the food and decided to give them some extra. Not thinking anything about the small amount of extra food given to them, there was a great surprise waiting for me the next evening.

When the next evening came, and it was once again time to put them in for the night, I drove over to her home and was amazed at what happened next. Getting out of the car and starting to walk toward the pen, I noticed an apparition next to her home. It was a female in spirit form radiating the beautiful light of her spiritual body. The color was not as bright and intense as I would normally see around those in spirit. Rather, it was simply a soft and soothing white hue around her. As she stood there faintly glowing, I recognized the apparition through Clair cognizance as Ruby. When viewing her, I could immediately sense her essence, the core of her spirit personality. She stood quietly looking at me while I looked directly at her. It was difficult to see what she was wearing, as the glow emanating from her body took priority. All I could see was the subtle glow around her body along with the gentle outline and features of her face.

How is it possible to recognize a spirit simply by viewing them? Many times a spirit can look quite different than they look or have looked in the physical sense. When seeing a person in spiritual form, either awake or during sleep, it is their essence that sets them apart. Our essence is our vibration at soul level. Since we are all individuals, each of us has a different spiritual vibratory energy. So when observing a person in spirit, I will sense who it is by the energy coming from them. It is possible to communicate with not only those that have passed, but also the spirits of those still living on Earth in the physical sense. All of us have a spiritual side, whether we are living on the earth plane of this side or living on The Other Side in Heaven.

As Ruby's spirit stood there looking at me, she telepathically impressed a thought. In the spiritual sense, thoughts are very real and for that reason, thought transference to another person is used. There are times a person in spirit can talk directly into my ear, but even when they talk in that manner, it is still the thought of the apparition that is coming through into my physical ear. They do not speak with their mouths like we do in the physical manner.

Standing there softly glowing, she impressed the fact upon me it was not necessary to give the geese so much food. Spiritually she had sensed I had given them a bit too much, and her spirit was concerned about that. It did seem she wanted me to feed them the amount that she had asked me to. She loved her birds very much and wanted everything done just right for them.

How is it possible that a person fifteen hundred miles away could sense that I had given her birds a bit too much food? That is one of the amazing aspects of our individual spiritual side. Our spiritual self is so much more alert and perceptive than our conscious mind in our physical body. Our spirit knows the truth about things, while our conscious mind can constantly get confused and muddled with the persistent routine of daily life.

Ruby came back from her stay with relatives saying she had a great time, and the trip was well worth it. Although her spiritual self had appeared to me making her request known about the food, I doubt her conscious mind ever knew she had made that trip. It is possible to have a strong connection between our physical mind and spiritual soul. But with most people, there is very often a strong disassociation between the two. Most of us are understandably too caught up with problems and routines of everyday life in a physical world to give our soul awareness much thought. Although there is normally a certain amount of disconnect between our physical and spiritual sides, it is still possible through determination and perseverance to gain a better connection between the two.

One other time Ruby called and said, "Could you drive me over to a church event Sunday evening?" Dad had recently passed, and I was trying my best to help Mom create a new life for herself. Since Ruby didn't drive and there was no public transportation out to this church event, she depended upon someone to drive her. So I quickly replied, "Sure, we'd be happy to take you. It sounds like it will be an enjoyable evening." I felt it would be good for both of them and was sure we would all enjoy it.

Sunday evening came and we drove the mile over to her house to pick her up. She was her usual good natured self and wearing her customary big smile, she once again made us feel very comfortable and at ease. The drive out to the church location took about fifteen minutes. During the ride, we had the usual pleasant conversation, filled with lighthearted chitchat. She was very excited about going to this event, so it was a pleasure to drive her. When we arrived, I noticed the service was going to be held in a large school multipurpose building, rather than the usual church. Many cars were quickly filling the good sized parking lot, but we managed to find a space fairly close to the building.

After entering the oversized building, I observed that the interior had the usual high walls and ceiling for a building of that type. The ceiling was possibly three stories high with some bleacher stands folded back on the sides. Although this gymnasium was obviously used by the school's athletic department for basketball and other events, on this particular evening it had temporarily been converted as a place to hold the church service.

Finding a place about midway from the front, we quickly sat down. As the chairs started to fill with children and adults, I felt a clairsentient feeling quite out of the ordinary. There was a feeling of great joy in the room, with everyone acting very happy to be at this gathering. Of course it is normal to see a lot of enjoyment at this type of event, but the happiness in the room that evening seemed to go beyond that. This joyfulness was different as it brightened the energies of the large multipurpose room, greatly lifting the mood of everyone there. I could sense something very special was going to take place that evening. But what was it, and what did this very distinct feeling of elation mean?

The church service started with the usual hymns and words from the minister, and at that point it seemed to be a very normal service. The great feeling of jubilation continued, and yet the actual progression of the event seemed customary. It was a nice service, but there was nothing particularly out of the ordinary happening. However, I kept wondering why there was such a special feeling in the air, and what was going to make this service more unusual than others?

My questions were answered about midway through the service. The minister started his sermon with people listening to his words, when unexpectedly breathtaking angels appeared around the tall walls of the room. It was a magnificent sight for me to perceive, and as the minister continued to speak, I couldn't help but be fascinated by these glorious beings that had come to join the service. They were clearly multidimensional and had come in from the higher realms. Their exact details were not specific to my eyes, and I could not see the fine points of their heavenly bodies. Instead, they were in a form and shape of soft radiating colors, without defined body characteristics. But my Clair cognizance and clairsentience clearly told me they were angels, and I was viewing the beings that have so often been mentioned throughout history.

One totally fascinating aspect of their appearance was their height. The interior walls of that building were quite high, and yet these beings took up the entire vertical height of those walls. It was very awe-inspiring to witness, but why were these angels so tall, soaring in height to the ceiling? I really don't have the answer to that, although I feel their towering appearance gave them a very strong and supreme presence in the room. Their height displayed their authority and true magnificence. These heavenly life forms had been sent by God, and they had come to watch over and protect everyone there that evening.

Facing the front of the large interior room, I noticed there were a number of angels very close to both the left and right walls. It almost appeared like they were "on the walls," and for some reason; the angels close to the left wall seemed to catch my attention more than on the right side. The reason for this could have been that we were sitting on the right hand side facing the front, and for that reason it was easier to view the angels close to the left wall. There must have been at least five or six of them on the left hand side, with their great height and width covering the entire wall. During the service, I never turned around to look at the wall behind us, so I had no idea if the angels were lining that wall as well.

Although no one else in the room seemed to notice these giant beings in attendance that evening, I knew everyone there could feel their glorious presence. I am used to seeing many things that people ordinarily don't see, so it was perfectly fine with me that I seemed to be the only one that could view them. While others were attentively listening to the sermon, I was diligently watching and studying the angelic forms.

During the minister's sermon, he briefly spoke about angels. I thought at the time, if those in the large multipurpose room could only see the angels that were actually with them during the service, they might have an entire new perspective on them. People would then be reassured that they are every bit as real as anything in the physical sense, and that they most certainly do exist.

Now I understood the very special feeling of great happiness and bliss among the people when walking into the auditorium that evening. The angels would be joining the service, and although others did not see them with their own eyes, they could sense the incredible joyfulness of their presence. The attendance of these splendid beings was felt by everyone, with the energies emanating from them helping to lift the vibrations of the room to very high levels.

It is extremely comforting to know that angels are here to help us in many different ways. They can help lift our mood when we are feeling low or can protect us from potential harm. There are many reasons they come to offer their assistance and support. All we have to do is ask for their help, and these breathtaking beings of light will be at our side in an instant.

12

April 29th, 1992

Back in 1992, a very unusual sixth sense occurrence happened. April 28th was a pleasant spring day with the cool winter rains having come to an end a month earlier. The air was fresh after months of intermittent rainy weather, and nature was putting on a beautiful show. There were many shades of greenery on the trees, and some fields were still filled with vibrant wild flowers. However, it was planting season in my part of agricultural California, with the fields quickly giving way to the plow in preparation of the growing season.

April 28th started out in a very normal way, but by evening it would prove to be anything but usual. Late in the afternoon, I suddenly remembered some outdoor pots that needed a drink of water. Quickly going outside and grabbing a hose; I gave the plants a needed drink. The dirt in the pots had become quite dry and following their dose of water, I promptly went back into the house.

Evening came and the sun finally set. It had been a pleasurable day, and the anticipation of more warm spring days ahead felt very satisfying. Suddenly without any warning, there was a strong feeling to look outside in the front. It was unclear why this sensation had instantly come, but the strong urge to look was there. Something was not normal outside, and I needed to find out what was causing this reaction within me.

Many times my senses are a bit like radar, and when something is wrong or not quite right, I will normally start to sense it and be aware of the new foreign energy. Feeling a bit of apprehension, the adrenaline started to course through my body. Maybe there was a stranger out in the front, or maybe something needed tending to. Whatever was causing this feeling of stress, it needed to be looked at and hopefully resolved.

I quickly got to the front door and opened it up; noticing that the evening sun was gone, but some daylight still remained with total darkness not yet having set in. While looking out the opened door and taking a quick glance outside, I was shocked at what I saw. Without even stepping outdoors, the very first thing I noticed was a large dark cloud in the sky over the house. It was very large and although it expanded for miles, it didn't appear as a normal cloud in the physical sense. This formation looked different, having a feeling of extreme gloom and negativity within it. It was the negativity that surprised and troubled me so.

Standing inside the opened door, I continued to study it. With some daylight remaining, it was possible from that angle to make out the size and characteristics of this strange formation. The front door looked out to the western sky, but it was also possible to see the northwestern and northern sky from that vantage point. Observing the formation, I noticed that although it was large, it did have an edge to it. From the front door, the edge appeared to be possibly six or eight miles off to the west and northwest. Beyond that point, the sky was clear, and it was possible to see the remaining daylight from the sun that had just set.

Most clouds normally have some type of texture to them with areas of varying thickness or different shades of coloring. But this cloud wasn't like that. It appeared very dark without any sort of texture to it, having a dark charcoal grey, almost black coloring. Although part of the coloring could have been due to the darkening sky, the feeling of the cloud was the most noticeable feature, having a very oppressive and menacing energy within it. It was almost like the cloud had been created and existed because of some form of negative energy. How could this be possible and why was it happening?

The earth plane does have both positivity and negativity. This is just the way it is since we are living on a plane where both types of energies exist. We come here to experience both forms of energies, and in the process of confronting the negative in our everyday lives, we will hopefully overcome it, replacing the negative with positive energies.

As I stood there observing the cloud, I couldn't understand why it had such a strong feeling of pessimism within it. It appeared to be quite low in the sky and wasn't that high, but because of the threatening feeling, it truly startled me. The formation was very puzzling, and it was baffling why a cloud would feel this way.

To further study it, I decided to step outside several feet from the front door. With the north wall of the house blocking my view to the south, it was only possible to observe the western, northern, and eastern formation of it. It looked like a dark circular blanket above the house that was maybe four or five thousand feet high above ground level. Beyond the cloud, it was possible to see the edges of remaining daylight on the horizon off to the west and north. At the time, I guessed the cloud to be approximately twelve to fifteen miles wide from west to east, with the northern edge of the formation about six or eight miles away. Those were the dimensions I thought of using Clair cognizance, the ability to receive information through sixth sense knowing.

Another characteristic of this intimidating sight was that it was moving in a slow but steady direction from the northwest to the southeast. It seemed to be traveling possibly twenty or twenty-five miles per hour, sensing that speed through clairsentience. As I stood there looking up at this menacing cloud cover, I wondered what it meant and why was it making me feel so dreadful?

After a few minutes of viewing the formation, I felt the best thing to do was get back inside the house. It felt very strange at the time to feel that, but the energies in that odd formation troubled me so greatly, I knew the best place to be was indoors. There was great danger in that cloud, and my instinct said that if the energies within it should descend to ground level, there would be huge problems. If that happened, it would be very unsafe to be outdoors. As I went back inside the house, the energy and the cloud were continuing to move to the southeast, and it did not appear to be descending at that time.

Apparently the bizarre energy cloud continued to move to the southeast, because once back inside the house, I slowly became more and more at ease. I knew through sense awareness the great danger that had been overhead seemed to be moving on. It was very fortunate that these forces did not come down to the ground in my location, since I knew without a doubt they would then create much chaos and disharmony.

The lower energies are the exact opposite of the higher energies. While the high energies create great feelings of love, harmony, and peace; the lower ones do the reverse. We do live in a dimensional plane where both types of forces exist. There is both the good and bad here on Earth.

The following day on the twenty-ninth, the verdict of the Rodney King trial in Los Angeles was announced. Los Angeles Police Department officers, who had been on trial, were acquitted by the jury. That afternoon a large group of people were protesting the trial verdict and within hours after that, violence started to take hold of that city. The violence that started on one street intersection quickly spread throughout different areas of Los Angeles. It was a difficult and devastating time for that city, but finally after numerous days; schools, banks, and businesses reopened. The disorderly riots had finally been restrained and silenced.

On the evening of the twenty-eighth when the dark energy cloud was appearing overhead, I never thought about the ongoing trial far to the southeast. At the time, I lived approximately four hundred fifty miles northwest of that area and through clairsentience, I felt the cloud of energy was traveling about twenty or twenty-five miles per hour as it headed in a southeasterly direction, directly toward Los Angeles. If the energy formation maintained that speed, it would have arrived in that area around the time the verdict was read. Shortly after the verdict was given, Los Angeles seemed to erupt into rebelliousness like a powder keg. After hearing about the uprisings on the nightly news, I thought to myself "At least now I know where the ominous cloud has settled; an area of Los Angeles."

There was no question in my mind in what I had experienced on the evening of the twenty-eighth. Viewing that intimidating cloud of energy was very real as it headed southeast. After hearing about the disturbances in Los Angeles, I then realized what I had seen on the evening of the twenty-eighth was paranormal. There was a physical cloud over my home, but it was obviously not going to physically travel to Los Angeles. However, it was a sign that discordant energies in the form of an energy cloud were headed four hundred fifty miles to the southeast. The sixth sense feelings that were inside the physical cloud were perfectly genuine, and my instinct knew that wherever it landed, it would cause great dissonance and discord among the people. That is precisely what happened starting on the afternoon of the twenty-ninth.

Although there was absolute certainty in what I had seen, normally there is some initial confusion whether it is sixth sense or not. Many times I can not tell if I am seeing something in the physical or spiritual sense, since the spiritual often appears every bit as real as the physical. It is only after the experience has happened that it becomes possible to sit back and analyze it, trying to understand exactly what has occurred. In this instance, it was obvious that physical clouds don't have feelings to them. But when the paranormal event is actually happening, I forget about logic and instead just concentrate on the event.

It is my belief that normally events will unfold on the astral plane and then come down to our physical level. Since the astral levels have no time as we know it, events are actually shown there before happening here on Earth. I was seeing with my physical eyes an energy that had done just that. It had already been reality on the astral level, and it was now on the physical earth plane headed directly for that area.

Would it have been possible to avert this negative disaster and the ensuing days of unrest? In short, I do feel the answer is a definite "yes." If we collectively as a group raise the energy level of a situation, I feel something like this could have been avoided. There was an understandable great amount of anger and frustration among some of the people in Los Angeles. When the verdict was finally announced, the emotional anger manifested into turmoil and rebellion. The dark energy cloud heading into Los Angeles could not have been avoided with the type of emotion many people were feeling.

However, this event could have been circumvented if everyone that had anger in their hearts had replaced it with more positive emotions. In fact, by raising the collective energy level, the outcome would most likely have been different, coming to a better conclusion for everyone. We do live in a world that has both good and bad, and we come to the earth plane to experience both types of energy. However, after experiencing any type of negative emotion, it is up to us to raise our own energy levels, replacing lower energies with higher positive ones.

The fact many people were caught up in the unrest means it was most likely written into their life charts as something that was going to happen to them. However, if the energies of that event had collectively been raised by everyone concerned about the trial, the civil disturbance would not have been written into their charts, and there would then have been no uprising that would have materialized. Without any upcoming disturbance, there would have been no ominous energy cloud headed to that area.

How do we go about raising our own energies or the energies of a situation or place? It really is a rather simple task, and there are two important ways to accomplish that goal; through thought and prayer. Thoughts are things, and this is something that is not yet widely understood here on the physical earth plane, but is very much understood on spiritual levels. In fact, thought projection on the spiritual side is one of the basic means of creating, traveling, and communicating with others. Since Earth is on a physical level, of course it is not possible to materialize something through thought or think of traveling somewhere in a physical sense, and instantly finding ourselves there. That is certainly not achievable in the physical way, but it is still possible to do on a spiritual level, sending out good thoughts with very favorable results coming back.

When we think about a situation, we are actually projecting that thought out into the atmosphere, and it will instantly travel to whatever we have thought about. Because of this fact, when we want to raise the energy level of something or someone, one good way to do it is to project positive thoughts. All thoughts of goodness, kindness, and unconditional compassion hold very high energies. These energies are the same type of energies that are found in the high realms of The Other Side.

If we confront a negative situation and actually project good thoughts to it, we are helping to lift the energy level of what we have thought about. Also, we are furthering our soul development, since the spiritual purpose of being here is to confront negativity, hopefully replacing it with positive resolve. When we project these good thoughts to something, we are helping to raise not only the energies of what we have projected to, but also our own vibration. We are elevating the vibration level of both the recipient and ourselves through our thoughts. Whenever we desire to elevate the energy level of a certain situation, all we have to do is put out good thoughts. It's as simple as that.

Another excellent way to raise the energy level is through prayer. Regardless of our religion or belief system, as long as we have love and sincerity in our hearts when praying, we are actually making an instant connection with the higher realms and the God Light of the spiritual side. This energy is composed of everything good and all things pure. Once this connection is made through prayer, we have created a strong and powerful link between ourselves and the magnificent God Light. When we make this request for help in any way, we are actually initiating the process of these most rarified energies going to the thoughts of our prayer. When we pray, it also greatly benefits us since we are the ones creating the connection with the God energies of unconditional love and purity.

When tuning into the high realms of The Other Side, I have always felt incredible joy and happiness from the people residing there. There is never a moment there that isn't filled with absolute bliss and contentment. They are wholeheartedly connected to the God Light, and that energy eternally shines very brightly on them. Although we do have negativity here on Earth, it is of course possible to connect with God's energy and the higher energies of The Other Side. Prayer is one excellent way to do that and when doing that, we can then experience a minute portion of the wonderful pleasure and joy that those on The Other Side always feel.

13

An Intuitive In Marin

A number of years ago, I had an acquaintance that I had met through another friend. Her name was Isabelle, and as our friendship developed, I discovered she was a delightful and charming person. Our camaraderie blossomed with each passing week and month. We had met by happenstance when the other friend had casually mentioned her, saying she was a nice woman, and that she was also a person having sixth sense abilities.

After she had mentioned the fact this person was an intuitive and psychic, it stirred my curiosity about her. I had always felt some fascination about other people having extra sensory perception and had wanted to form an association with them, since both of us would have that in common. Being used to many paranormal experiences, I wanted to feel a common connection with others that had similar occurrences. The spiritual world for me had always been every bit as real as anything in the physical sense, and I felt the desire to find others to talk with about the subject. Although I wanted to converse paranormal events, I had never found too many people that I could share those types of experiences with.

When my friend suggested that I meet this person I thought, "Meeting and conversing with Isabelle sounds intriguing." It was exciting and energizing to think about getting together with her, and it seemed like a great opportunity to chat, hopefully finding out more about her and what made her have this quality of extra perception. At the friend's suggestion, I called Isabelle, and we set up a time to get together.

The day came to drive over to her home in Marin County, north of San Francisco. On the way over, I was feeling a little bit of nervousness, wondering what type of person she would be and if we would make a friendship connection. I also wondered if I would say the right things and present myself correctly. Since I had very often kept my sensitive perceptions to myself, it seemed stimulating, but also a bit challenging, that I would chat with her on a one to one basis. However in retrospection, the two of us had much in common with our extra perceptive sensitivities, and the fact she was a pleasant person made it easy for a nice friendship to develop.

When arriving at her house, she answered the door with a big smile and hearty welcome, which immediately put me much more at ease. After talking with her a few minutes, I noticed Isabelle seemed to be a very warmhearted person, having a nice gentle demeanor about her. Walking through her house, a picture of a man on the wall caught my eye. The picture seemed to stand out in a certain way and sensing the man had a lot of significance to her, I casually asked who was in the portrait. Many times the spirit of the person in a photo or picture will come through, and that happened with this particular picture. I could tell there was some type of strong connection between Isabelle and this person, getting the impression the man was also an intuitive, since many times I will see it through the eyes.

Very often a person who experiences the paranormal will have a certain depth and intensity to their eyes, appearing deeper than average possibly due to the fact that they see things in a different way from the usual. They are seeing beyond the normal range of sight and his eyes were definitely saying this, as they had that certain strength and concentration within them. Also, the man's eyes seemed to come alive like he was actually with us at the moment, and he seemed to be observing us through that portrait. That is how I knew his spirit was coming through at the time.

As we started walking into the other room, she quickly explained that the man had been her teacher and had apparently given her some type of instruction on the paranormal world. I asked no further questions, and she volunteered no other information about him. But my first impressions were correct; he was very spiritually oriented, and there was a strong connection between the two of them.

On that first meeting, we had a very nice informal discussion. We talked about topics that were all spiritually related, and I listened intently as she explained extra sensory abilities from her perspective. Since I was used to my own private world of sixth sense experiences and had never discussed the topic with very many people, it was wonderful to chat with her, getting some of her viewpoints on the subject. As she continued to describe the psychic world from her own experiences, I sat listening, taking in all the information she discussed.

When it was time to leave we said our goodbyes, and I went home thinking of the nice talk we had that afternoon, contemplating the different spiritual topics that had been discussed. Our first meeting and chat had gone well. My friend was correct; she was a very compassionate and kind person. This meaningful friendship with Isabelle strengthened after our first visit together. However, there was a problem of the mileage distance between us, since we were a good hour's drive from each other. So instead of continually meeting in the physical sense, we would call each other and converse on the phone, always finding plenty to talk about.

After having created this friendship bond with Isabelle, I started to have some intriguing nighttime experiences during sleep.

Occasionally I would find my spiritual self with Isabelle, who was always busy conducting a class. During sleep, our individual spirit can leave the body, but we always stay attached to our physical body by a thread called the silver cord. This cord acts as a type of umbilical line between the physical and spiritual selves. The only time it is severed is upon death. At that time, it is automatically cut, and our spirit is free to permanently leave our physical body.

From personal experience, I have found it possible to visit a wide range of planes and dimensions during sleep. It has been possible to spirit travel to places right here on Earth, or journey to various levels of the astral plane, and even travel to the very high realms of light. So it is possible to travel to these various places while we sleep. Our spirit connected to our body by the silver cord can travel to these different planes of existence, and when our spiritual trip is concluded, we return back to our physical self.

Being together with Isabelle conducting her class, I was most likely visiting her on one of the astral levels and not the earth plane. It would also have been nighttime for her and she would not have been conducting a class that late at night. However, the astral plane has no time as we know it and is composed of past, present, and future combined. Events that show themselves on the astral plane can materialize on the earth plane. So it is entirely possible the class she was conducting while I was with her, would actually occur in the past, present, or future here on Earth. When I was with her, she did seem to be very aware of my presence, beaming at me with her usual warmhearted smile.

One day the friend that had introduced me to Isabelle called and said, "Let's go over and have brunch on Sunday with Isabelle and some of her friends." That sounded like a great idea, so I quickly said, "Sure, let's do it. That sounds enjoyable." We enthusiastically made arrangements to get together for brunch over in Marin County. When Sunday arrived, I met my friend at her place of business. She quickly got into my car, and we headed off for the restaurant, with both of us feeling very eager and excited about the morning car trip. On the drive over, we found a great deal to talk about, with both of us conversing nonstop.

Arriving at the restaurant, we located Isabelle and her friends. The group of us sat down for an enjoyable Sunday brunch, having a lighthearted and pleasant discussion. There was no talk about paranormal and sixth sense experiences, but rather the conversation was light and composed of casual chatter.

When the time came to leave, all of us headed out the door and stood in the parking lot saying our goodbyes. My friend and I were going to drive off in one direction, with Isabelle and her friends going in the other. While we stood chatting for a minute before departure, suddenly something very unusual happened. Isabelle started talking to me, but she wasn't talking in the physical sense. Rather, she was talking to me with her spirit using telepathy. While she was speaking in this manner, she didn't say a lot; just that it had been very nice to see me again and thanks for coming. What was additionally fascinating was that my spirit replied back to her, telling her it was real nice to see her, and to take good care.

Some people have called this "mind talk," and it is actually a form of telepathy we speak with on a spiritual level. Talking in this manner can sound just as if we were talking in the physical sense; however, it is being done through spiritual means and not in a physical way. Thought impression and telepathy are the main means of communication for our spirits since thoughts are things on a spiritual level.

As Isabelle and I said our goodbyes to each other in that way, the others continued to speak in the physical manner. They had no idea that the two of us were saying goodbye using telepathy. When speaking in this way, it feels likes an entire new method of communicating has opened up; the awareness of actually articulating here on Earth using our spiritual self to communicate rather than our physical mouth. I do think eventually thought impression and spiritual telepathy might be used much more here on Earth by all of us, and it could actually become quite commonplace, occasionally replacing the need to speak with our mouths. As we gain a deeper understanding of the connection between our physical and spiritual sides, this type of communication could be developed.

As time passed, Isabelle and I slowly lost touch with each other. I had moved away to a less urban area, so we became even further apart in miles. One time I called her from the new location, asking if she would like to drive up so we could get together for a chat. However, she replied that she was unable to come up at that time, but thanked me anyway for the invite. Despite the fact we lost touch with each other in the physical sense, the spiritual connection between us remained. Although we no longer called each other, there was still a friendship place in my heart for that special person in Marin County, and I'm sure she felt the same.

About a year after the last phone call to Isabelle, I was at home enjoying a routinely normal weekend afternoon. Everything seemed usual while going about the everyday schedule, when suddenly and unexpectedly, something very atypical happened. While walking into the bedroom, I suddenly looked toward the ceiling and clairvoyantly saw Isabelle. The clairvoyance of "clear sight" was quite fast and fleeting, which was a sign that it was coming in from the higher realms. Since the higher energies of The Other Side have a much higher vibratory level than here on Earth, information of any type will normally come through to the earth plane very fast. How did I immediately know it was her? It was through instant recognition of her essence, the soul of her spirit. After viewing the clairvoyance and sensing her essence, I immediately knew it was my good friend Isabelle. She appeared to be sitting in a seat that looked like a plane seat, and while she was sitting there, I watched as she ascended upward. During that time, she turned her head around while sitting in the seat and looked back at me, waving goodbye with a huge smile on her face.

Suddenly just as quickly as the clairvoyance had appeared, it was gone. Although it had only lasted a couple of seconds, the content of the psychic experience spoke volumes. Through Clair cognizance, or "clear knowing," I knew at once she had come to say goodbye to me, and that she was leaving the earth plane. She was at least thirty years older than me, so it was understandable that even though she was not that old, her time to leave the earth plane had apparently arrived. While watching her ascend upward, I received the thought impression that she was going to Heaven. She looked very pleased, and I sensed she was most content and at ease about her departure. I often think of that clairvoyance, and the fact she had wanted to let me know she was going home, returning to the wonderful high realms of light on The Other Side.

14

Light From The Other Side

During our phone conversation, my friend politely asked if I wouldn't go over to the hospital to see her husband. "Oh yes, I will go over there right now and see him," I quickly replied. She had been having an extremely hard time with her husband having been so sick for numerous months. My older friend had done an excellent job of taking care of him, but now with feelings of great emotional upset and physical exhaustion setting in, she found it very difficult to give him proper care at home. She had tried her very best to help him, but now found herself at the end of her rope both emotionally and physically.

The doctor finally agreed the best thing to do was to admit him to the hospital. His condition was getting worse, and it was time for specialized hospital care. There he could receive constant twenty-four seven attention, while she could get a much needed break from the stressful care giving that had been draining so much of her energies.

After his hospital admission, she was finally able to get more rest. Of course she was still very concerned about him, constantly going back and forth to the hospital checking on him and his latest condition. I was more than happy to go see him and felt it might make her feel better, giving her some peace of mind knowing that others cared a great deal. In addition, I would be able to have a little chat with him, hopefully giving him a boost of compassionate support.

Walking down the hospital corridor to his room, I was filled with different mixed emotions. It would be nice to see him, but I wondered how he would look health wise and how serious his condition would be. As I got closer to his room, those emotions within me built-up and intensified. It is hard to see a friend or loved one in that situation of deteriorating and poor health, but it would also be enjoyable to have the short visit with him.

After going through the door and entering his room, I was totally taken by surprise at what I saw. Expecting to see an ailing older man in very poor health, I instead saw something that fully shocked and astounded me. He was wearing a standard hospital gown, but my eyes were drawn immediately to his face. The very first thought that came into my mind after seeing his face was "He has the pureness and innocence of a child." In fact, I was so stunned when seeing that quality within him that I stood motionless, quietly staring and trying very hard not to show my feelings of surprise and awe.

It is my belief from personal observation that those in Heaven are eternally in the prime of their lives. Since there is no earth time in Heaven, everyone there is enduringly young. Although they can change their appearance much like we would put on a different set of cloths, their natural soul appearance is that of a youthful person in their prime. This is not something based on fiction and some imaginary tale, but rather based on my own experiences with those in the higher realms.

Another feature of these young looking people in Heaven is that they have a great quality of spotlessness and innocence about them, always reminding me of children. In fact, I have nicknamed them the "thirty year old children." Children have much purity and goodness within them, and I have also found the same qualities in the people residing in the higher realms. They might appear fully grown and in the prime of their lives, but God's pureness in their souls shines through with incredible radiance.

As I looked at the older friend lying in the hospital, I noticed he had no wrinkles. His face was pure and blemish free, with the wonderful bright glow of righteousness around his face. Needless to say, it was startling when expecting to see a failing person in very poor health, but instead entering the room and witnessing such splendor. Seeing that magnificent light around his face left me feeling totally awestruck.

Why did I see this and what did it mean? I feel the brilliant glow was his aura, the energy field which is around all of us, that was changing. Over the years, I have sometimes noticed before a passing, a person's aura will start to gradually change. As the energies of the physical body become weaker, the energies of the spiritual side start to increasingly dominate. At this time, a person about to pass will actually start becoming more spiritual and less physical, even though they still have not yet left the earth plane. The passing is inevitable and it will happen. However during this process, they are making the gradual transformation from the physical to the spiritual side.

Of course this can't happen when death comes fast and without warning. In those instances, a person can be very vital and alive on Earth one moment, and then they are gone the next. With those people, there is no time to make the gradual readjustment. I have often thought when a person has had a terminal illness that has lingered; they have actually been in the process of "growing to Heaven." They are slowly making the adjustment to their new body, and once the silver cord attaching the physical and spiritual selves is severed, the adjustment is complete.

Although I was expecting to see an older man very sick in the hospital bed, instead I had a glimpse of the wonderful body he was about to have. He was going to have a body that is always young and in the prime of life; a body that is always filled with the pureness and innocence of a child. He did live for another week after seeing him, and then he quietly passed over to the warm glowing light of The Other Side.

In another instance a similar type of experience happened. A very nice couple had stopped by my house. They lived in the area, and we had gone to the same church years earlier. After the visit with them, they got ready to leave and when walking out to the car with them, I noticed similar qualities in the face of this older male that I had seen with the friend in the hospital. When saying goodbye to them at the car, I noticed the face of the man appeared very young, looking about thirty years old. This was a man in his seventies or early eighties, and yet his face appeared as a young man in his prime.

Just like the older acquaintance in the hospital bed, this man also had a genuine childlike quality about him. The great virtuousness and pureness in his face reminded me once again of a thirty year old child, just like I had seen in the hospital. However at the time, I did momentarily forget about the experience in the hospital and was instead concentrating on what I had witnessed. After they were gone, I went back into the house feeling very confused; forgetting about the other male and not understanding how this man could appear so young. Normally when having a sixth sense experience, I just let it happen without stopping to think why it is occurring. After the incident has taken place, I can then start to analyze what has been experienced.

A few weeks later I received some surprising news. The man that had come visiting with his wife had suddenly become seriously unwell. Unknown to me at the time of their visit, this man did have a major health problem which suddenly got much worse. After becoming very ill, he told his wife he was ready to go home to Heaven. He was admitted into the hospital but was unable to overcome his health problems, passing away several days after hospitalization.

When hearing this news, I then fully understood why the man had appeared as an unblemished thirty years old with childlike spotlessness two weeks earlier. He was getting very close to passing, and I was simply seeing his growing connection between the high energies of light with his soon to have life on The Other Side.

The glow around the faces of both of these men was an extraordinary sight. It was very pure and emanated a wonderful light, radiating a feeling of great warmth and childlike compassion. In the higher realms of The Other Side, colors are very much different than they are here, having a depth and beauty to them that is not possible here on Earth. Since the senses tend to blend together there, it is not only possible to see breathtaking colors, but to also feel and experience them. Not only do the senses blend together there, but they are also infinitely magnified compared to the senses here on Earth.

I do believe the main reason sense awareness is so greatly intensified there is that God's light shines very brightly in the spiritual higher realms. There is no negativity there like here on Earth to make colors a bit duller and less vibrant. The purity and wholesomeness of those very high vibrations create these amazingly wonderful colors and warm feelings.

In yet a third instance, once again the higher energies started to increase in a person's aura before death, as the connection with The Light started to grow stronger. This man was younger than the previous two, but still in his sixties at the time. He and his wife lived in Lake County, the beautiful vacation resort area in Northwestern California. It was always fun getting away to Lake County for a few days on a weekend, enjoying the nice fresh country air and having some relaxation by the lake.

On one trip while vacationing in Lake County for a few days, this person came over to my cabin for a visit. He was a neighbor at the time, living several doors away from me. After the short chat, he was getting ready to leave when I noticed something unusual in his aura. Just like the other men, he appeared to be physically less dense with the higher energies of light around him. This was something that I had never before seen with this person, and in this particular case, I noticed the glow was not only around his face like the other two men, but it was also surrounding his entire body. The radiance wasn't as noticeable as it had been in the faces of the other two men, but although the glow was weaker than the other two, it was still there. The faint glow surrounding his body appeared to have some transparency, reminding me more of a male in spirit form than a physical man.

At the time, I didn't think a lot about what I was seeing. As was usually the case, I just let the moment of the experience happen without trying to figure out why it was occurring. Although the radiance was perceptible; it wasn't unusual enough for me to become totally amazed and shocked about. For that reason, I just forgot about it, not thinking anymore of the faint glow and hint of transparency around him.

Numerous months later some surprising news arrived; the neighbor man in Lake County that I had seen with the weak radiance around his aura had passed. I never found out exactly what his health issues had been that caused his passing. But it was a powerful surprise when hearing that news; since I had no idea his health problems were that serious.

After hearing of his passing, I immediately remembered the last time I had seen him with the weak glow and slight look of clearness around his body. It was then that I realized what I had seen that day up at the lake was his gradual transitioning from this side to The Other Side. His passing was imminent, and he was going to use an upcoming exit point that had been written into his guiding life chart. Because of this, he was merely starting the process of leaving the earth plane. As his earth energies started to weaken from the physical body, The Light from the higher realms started to make an appearance around him. The fact that the radiance and glow was a bit faint when seeing him was most likely due to the fact the actual passing was still numerous months away. When I saw him, his transitioning process was not as far along as the other two males. They were much closer to passing over, so their luminescence and glow was much brighter.

With all three men, a changeover process started to occur before they left the earth dimension. This gradual process was their progression of becoming ever closer to The Other Side, and each of them was in a transitional stage of exchanging their earthly body with a heavenly one. These men were simply making a gradual alteration, so they could leave this side and crossover to The Other Side.

15

Dimness Of The Gray Plane

During our lives, things sometimes happen to us that we wish wouldn't have happened. These errors just seem to be a part of life, an ingredient of the learning process and even a component of our guiding life charts. These events occur, very often coming upon us extremely fast and without warning. The old adage that "life is the best teacher," is many times a very true saying. There are times we do lack foresight, and a resulting situation does come about because of that negligence. If only we would have had more forethought on a potential predicament, maybe we could have avoided much upset and turmoil.

However, there are times that even if we did anticipate the potential problem, it would still come upon us, and there would be nothing we could have done to prevent it. Normally these things have already been written into our individual chart, and these events happen that way for a specific reason, for some type of personal learning process and soul growth.

Years ago a situation happened where I was lacking in forethought and because of the failure to think ahead of time about the potential outcome, I suffered for several years with major health problems. It was a warm summer's afternoon the year of that tragic incident.

I had decided to treat a wooden deck on my property with an oil based wood preservative. Using a hand held garden sprayer, I would spray the preservative onto the decking, first completing one section and then going on to the next one. Since it was a good sized area, I was spending quite a bit of time on the project.

The preservative contained a soup of various chemicals, which I was well aware of. However, in a great lack of prudence, I failed to take one very important precautionary step. I was wearing the standard protective gloves and even a dust mask to help prevent from breathing the fumes, but I failed to wear the correct type of shoes. Instead of wearing rubber or heavy material boots, I wore some thin cloth tennis shoes, which felt very comfortable and cool in the summer heat. That decision proved to be a very serious mistake.

While working on this project, I noticed the cloth shoes had gotten a little wet from the spraying. But again I gave it little thought, not stopping to realize the preservative loaded with chemicals was going right though the cloth fabric directly to my skin.

After the project was completed, I had a sick feeling within me, but it was still was not that bad or extreme at the time. However, as the days passed after that work project, I started feeling continually worse. It was a terrible feeling, and I didn't know what was wrong, but I did know something was definitely off base health wise. During that time, I never stopped to realize the small amount of oil based preservative that had been in contact with my feet was the reason for feeling so ill.

Everyday the situation deteriorated, as I constantly felt more disoriented, irritable, and nauseous. Then on the morning of August 10th, I went to get out of bed, but was unable to muster the strength to get up. It was a horrible feeling since I had always been a strong healthy man, but now for some reason there was no strength left in me, as I stayed quiet in bed looking up at the ceiling. It felt like a ton of bricks was lying on top of my body, pushing me down into the mattress and forcing me to stay motionless.

This severe chronic fatigue continued for numerous days, until I could no longer tolerate it. My healthy life had suddenly become a nightmare of health problems. Finally I went to the hospital and was immediately admitted. After a couple days of tests and some intravenous rehydration, the doctor released me to go home. All of the tests had come back normal except for one which showed elevated levels of Epstein-Barr virus in my system.

Epstein-Barr is a rather complicated virus. Apparently most people have been infected with it by the time they reach adulthood, but with most of us it remains dormant in the body. However, stress or environmental pollutants can activate the virus, causing a great deal of discomfort. This virus is also associated with Chronic Fatigue Syndrome, Human Immune Dysfunction, and other viruses.

From research at the time, I concluded what must have happened is that my immune system had become overburdened after the contact and ensuing absorption of the chemicals from the wood preservative. These introduced chemicals into the body set up a type of chemical poisoning, which greatly affected my entire system. Once the immune system was weakened and could no longer fight the invader well, the Epstein-Barr virus along with other possible viruses activated inside my body.

It was a miserable couple of years after the hospital stay. Chemical poisoning can be very dangerous, and I had received a large enough dose of the chemicals to become very seriously ill. My immune system was so overtaxed with that amount of dangerous compounds, it was impossible to function normally.

I fought a long and difficult battle to wellness, which took about three years. The road to better health was almost nonexistent for the first two years, seeing very little improvement at the time. During this time nutritional therapy was used, along with avoiding as many manmade chemicals in the air, food, and water as possible. My system was overtaxed and overloaded with chemicals, so I had to reduce, not add more, to my body.

After two years of struggling with this terrible illness, I was feeling physically worn down and emotionally drained. Despite constant everyday good foods, nutritional therapy, and exercise, the extreme health problem had taken a huge toll. Progress was very slow, and it felt like good health would most likely never return.

About two years after having this bizarre and dangerous problem, something very fascinating and uplifting happened. The start of the third year seemed to be the major turning point toward progressively improving health. However, immediately before that gradual improvement came; an interesting spiritual event took place.

One very special day after having been so sick for close to two challenging years, I was at home sitting in a chair trying to relax, when suddenly I saw my spiritual self using the clairvoyant third eye. Directly ahead of the chair about ten feet I viewed myself in another dimension, and through the sixth sense ability of clear knowing, realized it was my spiritual body that I was viewing. My spiritual side was in another dimension separate from my physical self sitting in the chair.

It is normal and characteristic for our spiritual side to separate from our physical body during sleep, as we astral travel to places on Earth or to other dimensions and planes. This type of travel is common, with our spirit always staying attached to the physical part of us by the umbilical tie of the silver cord. However, when viewing myself in this other dimension, I realized it wasn't the normal type of astral travel which occurs during sleep. Through Clair cognizance, I knew that my spiritual self had been separated from my physical side for a long time. In fact, it felt like it had been separated during much of the previous two years of terrible health. However, my spirit was still attached to the physical body by the silver cord, because if it had not been attached, I would not have been alive on Earth. Viewing my spiritual self in a place far different from the earth plane was remarkable to watch.

I have nicknamed this place "The Gray Plane," because that is what it reminded me of. Everything in that dimension was in different shades of gray, with no other colors anywhere in that place. The gray had a murky and foggy feel to it, and as I viewed this dimension through my clairvoyant third eye, I realized it was a plane of existence a little further away from The Light than the earth plane. The closer a plane of existence is to God's light, the brighter are the colors and higher the vibrations. This is why Earth has brighter colors and higher energies than this mysterious dimension I was observing, with nothing but gray colorings and energies. However, it is also why the very high realms of The Other Side have much more brilliant colors than on Earth.

This plane was nothing like Earth or the higher realms, because the energies seemed strangely dull and even lifeless. While sitting in the chair observing this dimension ten feet in front of me, I noticed this place was filled with many people in spiritual body form. They were all residing in their own small area of space within their own little world. There was no communication between anyone, and there was perfect silence and stillness everywhere. Then I realized I was witnessing a plane of existence that was some form of suspended animation. For whatever reason, the spirits of the people there were being held in a state of limbo, a plane where everything seemed to be frozen in time. It wasn't a bad place, but the gray coloring of that dimension gave it a somber and gloomy feel.

As I continued to watch, my spirit started to ascend, going ever higher and higher. There were people everywhere, and each cubicle of space seemed to be stacked one on top of the other. It reminded me of a giant high rise building, each floor composed of countless people, with each person inside their own compartmental space.

There were many floors to this high rise, at first seeing hundreds of people, and later possibly thousands. Floor after floor and story after story, I continued upward.

The people were not easily visible because of the grayness everywhere. They appeared much like silhouettes, with only their human outlines being seen. I sensed neither happiness nor sadness from them. Rather, they were simply in a state of suspension, being motionless and silent. At the time, I wondered what had happened in their lives to have caused this state of limbo for their spirits.

After several minutes of my ascension, the clairvoyance ended. Just as quickly as it had begun, it was over with. The image of the dull, dreary grayness ten feet in front of me was instead replaced with the normal familiar surroundings of the room.

Shortly after that sixth sense experience, my health started to make a major change for the better. Instead of everyday struggling with debilitating health conditions, I started having more and more days with improving health. Within months and much to my delight, the road to recovery was advancing nicely.

I am positive the clairvoyance in the room that day was the viewing of my own spiritual body exiting that dimension and reuniting with my physical self. Whatever that plane of existence is, I left it that day. Where had my spirit been and why had it been there? In retrospect, I feel it had everything to do with the severe illness. For two years, my body and mind was in a complete state of confusion and limbo, not even knowing if I would pull through or not. Everyday had been a constant challenge to keep from getting even worse, and under those conditions, it is understandable that my spirit would also have been in a state of deep conflict and limbo. It did seem reasonable that my spiritual self would go to a place where it could be quiet and suspended in time, waiting for the physical body and mind to hopefully start its major recovery. Within a year after that experience, I had once again regained good health. It had been an incredible challenge to recapture that strength and vigor, but it was most rewarding in the end.

Regarding the multitudes of people in that gray dimension; I feel prayer and positive thought greatly benefit them. Their spirits are in a deep confused state of limbo, in a place of total grayness, stillness, and silence. Prayer and positive thought are the great up lifters, and there are extremely high energies in both. If these energies are sent to those people in spiritual form, it is possible the force of goodness might break through the gray stillness. If enough of us send positivity to them, the collective higher energies they receive might be enough to help some of their spirits depart from that place.

I am positive that in addition to a program of nutritional therapy and exercise, the uplifting energies of prayer and positive thought sent to me during that prolonged illness helped greatly in my getting well. Those factors allowed my spiritual and physical sides to once again reunite, so I could then resume an active and fulfilling daily life on the earth plane.

16

Heaven's Close At Hand

After calling Marjorie on the phone one early afternoon, I enthusiastically said, "I'll be over in about thirty minutes for a short visit." Hurrying around the house, I promptly got ready for the five minute drive over to their home. It would be nice to see both of them, having a little chat filled with interesting conversation and joviality.

In life, there are some people we meet that we instantly like and quickly have a longing to better know. Once in a while, those types of people do come along, and Marjorie and Don were those kinds of people. As soon as I met them, I quickly felt a connection of camaraderie with them. They were good people, always glad to see me with a warm heart and welcoming smile on their faces. Although they were older than I was, the age difference didn't matter to our relationship. We became best of friends despite that fact, always enjoying each other's company and looking forward to the next visit.

During our conversations, we would always find a wide variety of things to discuss. With both of them being so much older, it was fun listening to the wisdom of their words as they spoke.

They had lived much longer than I had and had acquired a great deal of knowledge over the years to share with me.

As the years passed, Marjorie's health started to slowly decline. It was a gradual process, but eventually she found herself having some short hospital stays for various health related problems. Although this was difficult to watch take place, it is something that of course just happens with the aging process. We are living on a plane of existence that has past, present, and future. Time here is not eternal and because of that fact, aging is very much a part of life on the earth plane.

One spring day I went to their home for a chat, but Marjorie was unable to visit. Not feeling so well that day, she stayed in her bedroom resting while I spoke with Don. We had the usual nice chat and dialogue, with both of us fully enjoying the visit. Although it would have been nice to have seen her that day, it was still pleasurable being with him.

When preparing to leave, something very fascinating and spiritual took place. On the way to the front door, I happened to glance down the hallway where the bedroom was. It was not possible to see the bedroom door from that location in the living room, since the door was not in my line of sight. However, when glancing down the corridor, I suddenly had a clairvoyant image of Heaven. It was very fast and fleeting, which is normal when any type of information comes in from the high dimensions. With energy being so much lighter and moving so much faster in the high realms than here on Earth, clairvoyance will come through to the earth plane very swiftly.

Even though this third eye clairvoyance came in rapidly, I was still able to experience a great deal from it. When something comes through to me from these high places, it is almost like time stands still. Yes, it happens fleetingly fast in earth time, but it's as if that instant moment is suspended in time in the high realms.

This would be due to the fact that their time is so much different than here on Earth. With time as we know it in Heaven being nonexistent, everything there is simply measured in the moment, by the experience, and in an eternal atmosphere.

When being shown a glimpse of Heaven that day looking down the hall, I realized how breathtaking and glorious that place truly is. During the mental clairvoyance, I captured an infinitesimal amount of the radiance of that dimension. It is comparable to Earth in that there are grasses, trees, and flowers, with the topography appearing very similar to here. However, what makes Heaven so different from Earth are the extremely high energies. God's light shines very brightly there, and without any form of negativity, everything is literally perfect. There is an eternal euphoria to the place, a type of happiness and bliss that is not known here on Earth. I also sensed the great warmth that fills the dimension of Heaven, with a feeling of unconditional love that fills the air and permeates everything there. Every tree, flower, and person in Heaven can feel this love, since it is literally everywhere and in everything.

Throughout my life, I have noticed that this high realm is actually very close to the earth plane. From my observation as a psychic and intuitive, it is literally another dimension superimposed directly on top of us, with the veil between the two planes being very thin. What sometimes makes Heaven seem so far away is the great difference in energies between here and there. Earth is much denser with slower energies, while that realm is filled with great light and high energies that radiate to everything in that plane of existence.

During psychic clairvoyance looking down the hallway, I did sense that the energies of Heaven were starting to come around Marjorie. In the distant future, she would start "growing" to Heaven, making the gradual adjustment from this plane to that one. During this period of transition, she would remain on Earth until the time came for the silver cord to be severed. Although it could be months or even years away, her future destination of going home to that wonderful place was shown to me.

After that extra perceptive experience, her health gradually continued to deteriorate. Although she outwardly looked fine, she was no longer ambulatory. Unable to walk, she now spent her time in bed, taken care of by her loving husband.

About sixteen months after having the clairvoyance of Heaven in their home, I was working outside around my house and instantly experienced sixth sense clairsentience and Clair cognizance. Clairsentience is the ability of "clear feeling," when out of the blue, we suddenly feel something physically or emotionally, sensing without a doubt that it is the truth. Clair cognizance is the ability of "clear knowing," when we suddenly know something to be correct when there is no logical explanation as to why we know it.

At that time working outdoors, I suddenly felt the urge to look at some shade under a tree. It was still summertime and the shade looked very cooling and inviting. While glancing at the patch of coolness under the tree, I instantly sensed it applied to Marjorie. Through clairsentience and Clair cognizance, I knew without a doubt she was going to be passing soon, and felt the coolness of the shade meant her passing would be at the very tail end of summer, with the sun still warm but the shade quite cool. I could actually feel the coolness of the shade on my skin, despite the fact I was in the hot sun. This paranormal experience had come totally out of the blue, which was not surprising, since that is the way these events normally happen to me.

After experiencing that, I was deeply saddened knowing a special friend was going to be leaving the earth plane. However, I knew in my heart it was God's will, and there was nothing that could change what I had just felt and experienced. I was very happy for her, knowing she would be going home to a wonderful place;

but it is always hard to see special people in our lives leave in the physical sense.

About six weeks after that incident, I got up one morning and felt the impelling urge to go see my special friends Marjorie and Don. The urge within me was actually clairsentience, and I could physically feel the need to go see them, just as if someone were standing behind me pushing me toward the door. A second clairsentient feeling accompanied the first one, which was one of a major change about to commence. Why was there such an urge to see them at this time, and why was I feeling a major change was about to occur?

When I got there, Marjorie was resting comfortably in bed, so Don and I went outside to sit in the shade of the late morning sun. Since it was now the first part of October and the tail end of summer, the shade felt cool at that time of morning, with the intense heat of summer now gone.

While sitting there, I suddenly noticed a female in spirit form hovering slightly above the ground about ten feet away from us. Her actual body features were rather indistinguishable as the colors radiating from her body predominated. However through Clair cognizance, I knew without a doubt it was Marjorie. As I sat there watching the incredible colors of energy emanating from her, I also knew she was very close to making the final transition to the higher realms of The Other Side.

The colors which radiated from her that day are of course unlike any colors we have here on the physical level. They are composed of a multitude of various shades and hues, which softly glow and carry a great feeling of warmth and love. It was truly a heavenly aura around her spiritual self I was witnessing. She had left her physical body for a few minutes, and I feel she appeared in front of us to let me know she was about to go to her heavenly home.

Of course I said nothing about the apparition in front of us.

To mention her spirit appearing close to us would have been very inappropriate. As an intuitive and sensitive, I must always respect other peoples' feelings and thoughts, and it would have been very insensitive to have said anything about it at the time.

After leaving their home, I had a strange empty feeling within me. I knew her passing must be getting very close, as the colors around her spiritual body were so effervescent and heavenly looking. Immediately before a passing that has come on gradually, there seems to be a very strong interconnection between both the physical and spiritual sides for the person about to pass. It's as if they figuratively have one foot in both places at the same time. They are in the process of making the final change from this side to that one, waiting for the silver cord that connects their physical and spiritual bodies to be severed.

About nine that evening on the same day I had gone to their house, I received a phone call from Don. He called to tell me that Marjorie had passed several hours earlier, having gone quietly without any pain or discomfort. The silver cord had been cut, and her spiritual body was now free to step over to The Other Side. Upon hearing this news, a flood of mixed emotions coursed through my body. I felt at peace that she was able to go to her heavenly home, but the emptiness of knowing a very good friend had left the physical world was devastating.

When the day of the funeral arrived, I was feeling totally miserable, having come down with a bad head cold. My body was full of discomfort, with every cough and sneeze reminding me of the physical loss that I, along with all of Marjorie's family and friends, was feeling. After the service, I quickly said goodbye to various people in attendance and quietly left. Feeling so sick with congestion, all I wanted to do was go back to my house. A meal was being served after the service, but I felt much too uncomfortable to sit and visit with people.

After returning home, I quickly changed clothes and started to robotically putter around the house, trying to find something to do that might help keep my mind occupied. The congestion seemed to be getting worse, and I found it difficult to do much of anything except sit down and rest. Thoughts continued to flood my mind of the many good visits and fun moments of laughter I had experienced with Marjorie and Don. Lost in those thoughts and feeling so sick with bad congestion, I had forgotten to check the phone messages when arriving home. After remembering to check, I promptly got up and went to the phone, wanting to see if anyone had called.

There was one new phone message that had come in during the funeral service, so I mechanically pushed the button to see who had called. What happened next is one of the real mysteries of spirit. Throughout my life, I have had spirit send communications in so many different ways. It seems they are always finding new and special ways to get their messages across, and sometimes these ways are totally astounding and surprising.

When the phone message came on, I could hardly believe what I was hearing. It was Marjorie, sounding very normal in her everyday speaking voice. Her vocal inflection and tone was exactly like the voice she had here on Earth during her later years. She spoke only three words, but those words gave a very significant message, when she simply said, "I love you." The first two words came through very loud and clear, while the third word started to quickly fade out. Although I could still distinguish the word "you," it was clear her energies coming through the phone message had quickly lessened by that time.

Only that short phrase was spoken, then suddenly her voice was gone. After hearing the heartfelt message, my first feelings were one of amazement and wonder. That message had not been on the answering machine before the funeral, and yet sometime during the service, her spirit used the phone as a means to send the communication. What a wonderful and powerful way for her to get her point across to me. Listening to that message over and over, I thought of the many wonderful visits we had shared together, and the fact she had wanted to send her loving wishes.

How was it possible for her spirit to use the phone and to actually verbalize her earthly voice? My feeling is that immediately after a person passes, a strong physical link remains with Earth for a limited time. The silver cord has been cut, but because they have just lived on the earth plane, the strong memories of that physical life are still with them. They easily remember and continue to sense what physical existence on the earth plane was like. Once they have made the full readjustment to their new life in Heaven, many times it becomes a bit harder to do this type of powerful communication, as they gradually loose the awareness and feelings of physical life. However, I never rule out the many different ways spirit can correspond with us over time. It does seem if they want to get a message across, they will find some way to do it at any point in time.

One factor that plays a role in spirit communication is the amount of receptiveness in the recipient. If we are open and receptive to that world, it can make the contact much easier for them. Placing our thoughts and energies on the goodness and purity of the high realms helps to create a stronger link between them and us.

One of Marjorie's favorite colors was purple. She was definitely a "purple person" here on Earth, enjoying clothing or any other item having that particular shade of coloring. On two separate occasions several years after her passing, I was sitting watching television when suddenly a shade of purple appeared on the screen. The first time it happened, I noticed the right side of the screen was entirely purple. Immediately becoming concerned that something was wrong with the TV set, I held my breath hoping it would be ok, therefore preventing the purchase of a new set. Only the right side of the screen had this problem, which I found very odd. Why would the right half of the screen have purple coloring while the left side remained perfectly normal?

While continuing to study and observe this strange occurrence, I noticed that after blinking my eyes, the purple coloring started to fade. Out of curiosity, I started blinking my eyes quite rapidly, and to my surprise, after every blink came additional fading. It was then that I realized the purple tone on the right side of the screen was a vision. Clairvoyant visions with the physical eyes are so real for me; at first I don't realize that it is a vision. Looking every bit as authentic as something in the physical world, it is only after I have seen it and with logical reasoning, that I realize a vision has just taken place.

This particular vision lasted about two minutes and then left, fading away until all of the purple hue had vanished. After it was gone, I realized it was simply a sign from Marjorie letting me know she was thinking of me, and that she had found yet another way to communicate.

A similar type of experience transpired months later, and on that particular day I felt her presence around me in a very strong and definite way. This is possible since our friends and loved ones in Heaven do occasionally come down to the earth plane for a very brief time. They can come around us, checking to see how we are and to let us know they are thinking of us. Later that day after having sensed Marjorie, I turned on the TV set, and for a second time a vision appeared. On this second occasion the purple coloring was deeper, appearing on the top part of the screen. When seeing the purple hue on the top of the screen, I once again tried blinking; wanting to see if that would fade the vision. However, this time it was colorfast and refused to fade, so I eventually turned off the TV. When turning the set back on, the vision was gone.

It is truly wonderful that spirit can find so many ways to

communicate with us. The phone message and both visions of the purple coloring on the screen clearly told me it was Marjorie, and that she had simply wanted to say "hi" in a very unique way. Even if we don't often receive such strong definitive messages from those in Heaven, they can still communicate to us in a wide variety of subtle ways. Maybe it's the wonderful pleasant feeling we suddenly experience when thinking of a passed over loved one. Or it can be something occurring during our daily routine that clearly reminds us of a special person that has departed the earth plane. We can be so thankful that our friends and loved ones in the high realms think so highly of us, that they desire to keep the bond of unconditional love eternally open between them and us.

PART III

17

Sky Visitors

For a couple of years, I had an impulsive fascination with unidentified flying objects, more often known as UFO's. Maybe part of the attraction of that subject came from having had so many unusual sixth sense experiences. UFO's in my mind seemed every bit as fascinating as the constant paranormal occurrences of seeing, hearing, and knowing things. During those two years, I would often ponder and contemplate that subject, wondering if there truly was spacecraft from places beyond Earth, having been created by some sort of intelligence. My mind would often work overtime as I would think, "What type of energy powers those strange objects, where do they come from, and why are they visiting us?"

This topic has remained a very controversial subject by many people. Some people scoff at the thought of spacecraft from other worlds flying overhead, while others take it much more seriously and believe there must be some credibility to their existence. Years ago when feeling this fascination with the topic, I held a neutral opinion. If they existed that was fine, but if they didn't that was ok as well. Back then I looked at photos taken of these mysterious objects and read various stories about them. After doing some research, I would often wonder how many of those photos and stories were authentically genuine, while how many others were totally bogus? I speculated that if only one photo or one story was truthful, that would prove the existence of these craft. It would only take one true sighting to change the question of their possible reality to one of actual proof of their existence.

After studying the subject, I decided to hypothesize the theory that these spacecraft were real, and that they were controlled by intelligence. Assuming that hypothesis, I began to speculate if it could be possible to get in touch with that intelligence, reaching out to them through telepathy. As bizarre as that seemed, I knew my life had been filled with many unusual and curious events, with paranormal occurrences being just a part of my everyday routine. The idea of reaching an intelligence controlling these objects through thought transmission seemed a little bizarre even by my standards, but it was worth a try.

Using the supposition that UFO's were very real, I started placing mental thoughts out to the cosmos. As those thoughts were sent out, I requested that these unidentified flying objects reveal themselves to me. I wanted to know if they were real and if these objects were indisputably authentic and controlled by an advanced intelligence, possibly that intellect should be able to pick up on my thoughts.

Days and weeks went by as I occasionally but persistently continued placing those thoughts out to the universe. After weeks of doing this, I began to have clairsentient feelings regarding the telepathy. It felt like the thoughts had gotten through to some sort of intelligence, but the intellect at the receiving end felt very different from the earth plane and even the familiar heaven plane. The intelligence at the other end of the telepathic messages was real, but their thoughts seemed foreign to me, and I couldn't understand the awareness I was feeling. All I knew is that it certainly felt like someone or something had picked up on my thought transmission.

One evening weeks after having received the feeling that the telepathy had reached some intelligence, I went outside the house for a few minutes. The sun had set hours earlier, and darkness had firmly settled into the nighttime sky. Standing on the drive, I suddenly heard a clairaudient voice giving a very short but clear message. At the time, I couldn't tell if the voice was male or female, which was unusual, since most of the time it is possible to quickly determine the gender of the spirit giving the message. This voice simply said, "You're being observed." Within one or two seconds after hearing that, I immediately looked up into the night sky, to the exact position of a lighted object which at first appeared as a bright star. How was it possible to instantly look at the pin point location of that object when my eyes could have gone to anyplace in the vast nighttime sky? I don't have an answer to that, unless it was clairsentience or Clair cognizance, allowing me to immediately spot the exact position of this object in the darkened sky.

At first it appeared motionless as I stood there studying it, but after closer observation, it did seem to wobble slightly from side to side. Another interesting feature is that it was a cloudy night, and this craft was beneath the clouds. There was a moderately low solid cloud cover, so that ruled out any possibility it could have been a star shining through the clouds. Puzzled and mesmerized by it, I continued to watch this strange phenomenon in the darkened sky. Initially it appeared white looking very similar to a star, but within about one minute it turned to a bluish cast, with what looked like a red tail of fire on one end of the object. Seeing this was amazing, and I quickly came to the realization it must be a UFO.

There was a friend staying in my home at the time and wanting someone else to see what I was witnessing, I quickly went back inside to get him. "You're not going to believe this," I told him with anxious excitement, explaining to him there was a UFO in the sky, and I wanted him to see it. He didn't seem too excited, but hesitantly did start to follow me out the door. I got back to the driveway before he did, but then noticed the object was quickly changing back to a whitish hue and once again looked like a bright star. By the time he got to the driveway, it had completely changed back to white. He made a quick glance at the object, shaking his head and then quickly going back inside thinking it was merely a star. In fact, I could hear his thoughts, and he was a bit annoyed I would ask him to come out and see a star.

It was startling to realize the craft seemed to have some type of direct consciousness with me and didn't want others to see what I was witnessing. Apparently the object knew someone else was about to view it, so it quickly disguised itself, once again looking like a star. How was this possible that I would be told I was being observed, to instantly know the exact location of the object, and then to have the object disguise itself so another person couldn't see it? It really was a mysterious and baffling occurrence. Not wanting to take the time to go back into the house and explain that this craft was beneath the solid cloud cover, I stayed outside to observe it, feeling very spellbound wanting to see what would happen next.

Once again when I was alone, this mysterious craft started to resume a bluish tint. The intensity of the blue seemed to pulsate between a very light blue or almost white shade, back to a darker bluish cast. The red tail once again appeared on one end of the object, looking for a second time like a tail of fire. Stunned and fascinated, all I could do was continue to watch as this extraordinary sight went on for several more minutes.

Finally in an instant, the object suddenly started moving in a very fast upward trajectory. Its stationary position had been in a northeasterly direction from my location, approximately fifteen degrees off of meridian, the highest point in the sky. Rather than going straight up into the nighttime sky, its straight line of ascent appeared to have a very slight southerly angle. The velocity of the craft was amazing as it went from a stationary wobbling position to a high rate of speed within a second or two. In two or three seconds, it had gone through the cloud cover and was gone from sight.

What a remarkable thing to observe. I was stunned that the UFO seemed to be very aware of my presence; feeling like the connection between us was very strong. Once it was gone from sight, the experience stirred many questions in my mind. I began to wonder, "Where had it come from, what type of technology controlled it, and why was I able to see the object when my friend was not allowed to?"

After thinking about what had happened, I then remembered the telepathic messages that had been sent out for weeks to the universe, and the ensuing feeling that I would witness an unknown craft. Those messages had been sent requesting the reality of UFO's; if they were indeed real, it was my hope they would make themselves known to me. After this experience, I now had visual confirmation that my desire to know the truth of their existence had been reached by some sort of intellect, and that intelligence was simply answering my request.

Later that year, a second incident transpired involving a mysterious craft. It was early autumn and there was still some lingering summer warmth in the air, although much cooler weather was quickly approaching. For two or three weeks, I constantly had a knowing that I would be seeing another UFO. It felt like someone or some type of energy was frequently alerting me to the fact it would be taking place in the near future. The feeling was very strong and powerful, and I knew without a doubt it would happen.

One afternoon that fall while standing on the driveway by the front lawn of my home, I looked out to the ridge of hills one mile directly to the west. These hills were good sized, having numerous peaks and dips to them, running in a southeast to northwest direction. Traveling at a moderately slow but constant speed, I noticed what at first appeared to be a small plane flying directly above the ridge. Upon closer observation, I noticed it was a round object and looked nothing like an airplane, since it had no wings and lacked the familiar shape of a small plane. The afternoon sun was glistening on it, giving it a silvery sheen appearance.

As I watched, this object continued to fly over the ridge at a constant rate of speed, slowly and methodically staying in a straight-line course. Suddenly above the ridge possibly one mile directly ahead of the craft, a tiny round cloud appeared. This little cloud, being so small and insignificant, at first gave the appearance of a small round puff of vapor in the sky. However, it abruptly started to grow, quickly becoming larger and expanding its size outward in all directions. As it grew, it became much more noticeable, looking like a small puffy cloud in the late afternoon sky. I found it very strange that this was the only cloud around, since it was a perfectly cloudless sky that day. There were no other clouds anywhere, except this one mysterious formation that continued to grow directly ahead of the approaching shiny object.

As the silvery UFO got ever closer to the growing cloud, it looked like the object's straight-line path would fly it directly into the puffiness. After about a minute's time at the most, that very thing happened, and the craft did indeed fly into the cloud. By this time, the puffy white formation had grown from a tiny speck in the sky to a good sized smaller cloud. When the craft entered that formation, something truly incredible took place; it flew into the cloud and never came back out. Instead of the UFO coming out on the other side, the solitary cloud began to slowly dissipate, amazingly starting to break up and dissolve in front of my own eyes. It looked like the cloud formation had swallowed up the craft, and now it was thinning and dissolving.

As it started to dissipate and thin, another very intriguing thing took place; the cloud continued to further expand outward. Before the craft had entered, it had appeared as a small area of vapor that had grown to a normal small sized cloud. But now that the craft had entered inside this formation, it not only continued to expand, but it also started to enlarge and move toward where I was standing.

Awestruck with what was taking place, I watched as the thinning cloud started to take on the appearance of fog, all the while continuing to slowly drift toward me from its location above the ridge. Slowly but steadily the fog floated down to where I was standing on the driveway. Gradually it fully enveloped me, until all of my surroundings were in a foggy haze. Looking at my front lawn and the homes across the street, everything was in this mysterious fog. Not knowing what to do, I stood motionless and continued to observe the visual effects of the fog vapor, feeling no fear or upset from it.

For possibly five minutes, this heavy mystical vapor surrounded me, and then it further dissipated and thinned. It was a gradual process, but after several minutes of additional dissipation the air finally returned to normal. Once again all of the surroundings appeared typical with no traces of the foggy atmosphere anywhere.

My life has been filled with so many unusual experiences, that I really didn't think too much about this incident. It certainly was remarkable and mystifying to experience, but at the time, I simply accepted the occurrence with never any doubt as to what had happened.

Looking back on these two UFO sightings, I had initially wondered if they could have been visions. Clairvoyant visions are very real for me and can appear every bit as genuine as anything in the physical world. Yet in both of these cases, I came to the conclusion they weren't visions. Through clairsentience, I do feel both times there were two unidentified flying objects that were right here on the physical earth plane. However, it seems the intelligence that controls these objects has an entirely different technology and set of physics than we have here on Earth.

With the first sighting, the intelligence had the ability to access my consciousness and awareness, being able to communicate with me on a one to one basis. I was also able to observe the craft while my friend was not allowed to. As experienced with the second sighting, somehow the object had the ability to travel between Earth and another dimension, just like we would travel from point A to point B in a plane. Our spirit can travel to the astral dimension and higher realms during sleep, yet this intelligence appears able to dimension travel in a physical manner.

With the second occurrence, I do feel the UFO was physically real flying above the ridge. I have no idea if anyone else could see it or if this manifestation was exclusively for my eyes and awareness. Although I do believe it was there in a physical sense, the craft was able to go into the single cloud and literally disappear after all traces of the cloud and fog had dissipated. Somehow it physically dimension traveled from this plane of existence to another.

After these two experiences, I stopped putting out telepathic messages to the universe with a desire to know the reality of unidentified flying objects. Those two incidents proved to me that we are definitely not alone. Whoever they are or wherever they come from, I believe someday they will show themselves to the entire world. It would be a life altering event for all of us on this planet, and someday it should happen when we are better prepared and accepting of such major world change. After stopping the telepathic messages out to the cosmos with a request to know of their existence, I never again witnessed another UFO.

18

A Place Called Paradise

After I had asked Mom how she was feeling, she replied with dull enthusiasm saying, "I am fine." Although she might have said she was doing satisfactory, I knew in reality she really wasn't too well. For years her physical health had gotten worse, until it had finally reached a point where she was simply no longer healthy. Her numerous ailments were related to advancing age, something that happens but is certainly not welcome and wanted at the time.

For years, I had done everything possible to watch over her, giving her a helping hand whenever she needed one. Numerous years earlier, Dad's spirit had spoken to me before his passing, asking that I be there for her, and that I do everything achievable to keep her life as comfortably pleasant as possible. His spirit had told me at the time that he was going to be passing shortly, and this was his request after he had left the earth plane. Always having done what spirit has asked, I would never refuse this particular appeal. For that reason, I made his request a top priority in my life, always desiring to give her any needed support and guidance. Both my astrological and life charts also stated this fact, that there was dutiful responsibility within the family, and that responsibility was just part of this life's calling.

Although Mom had enjoyed many healthy years when younger, things were now different, with her ailing health giving the entire family cause for concern. However, with the advanced age she had reached, only so much could be done medically, and it was now time to keep her as comfortable as possible with the remaining time left.

Most families have experienced this type of difficult situation, and our family was no exception. Each of us within the family was trying to cope in our own way with the hard and trying circumstance. I was feeling emotionally and physically exhausted having become her caregiver during the last year of her life, and the constant stress had also been hard on everyone in the family.

The season had finally changed from late summer to early autumn. One afternoon I needed a few food items, making a fast car trip over to the grocery store. With her health situation, it was not possible to leave her for more than a very brief time, since she did require round the clock care. However, the grocery store was very close by, and when getting to the store, I quickly made a mad dash through the aisles buying the needed food items. Just as rapidly, I then got back into the car, feeling the need to swiftly rush back and check on her condition.

Starting the quick trip back, I noticed the female driver in the car directly in front of my vehicle. When looking at the female, I immediately received a thought impression from spirit. Thought impression is one of the primary ways the people in Heaven communicate to us. Since thoughts are things on the spiritual side, there is no need to communicate using the physical mouth. That is something that is only done here on Earth. Occasionally spirit will actually send the thought impression through clairaudience, or "clear hearing," directly into my ear. However, much of the time it is done through telepathic messaging directly into my thought process.

The message in the car that afternoon was one of both thought impression and clairvoyance. When seeing the female driver, I received the telepathic message that "A female will start going toward Heaven." Along with the message, I clairvoyantly saw the female directly ahead of me as if she were going upward toward Heaven. Of course nothing was happening to her in the physical sense. She continued to drive in a normal manner as I was shown the sixth sense image of her gradual upward ascent. At the time, little reflection was placed on the message, since my main concern was getting back to check on Mom's condition.

The next morning, I once again went over to the grocery store for a couple more items. When turning the corner at the end of the street, spirit continued with the thought impression from the previous afternoon. This part of the message came through as "between the dry and the wet." Putting the two parts together, the entire message now became, "A female will start going toward Heaven between the dry and the wet."

After receiving the second part of the message, I never stopped to think what it might mean. Of course I should have realized through clear knowing that the two combined messages were in reference to Mom. However, deep down I didn't want to accept or acknowledge that fact, and because of that conscious feeling, I refused to think about it, most likely shutting down any incoming Clair cognizant information pertaining to that particular message.

Autumn slowly turned into early winter, and Mom's health continued to deteriorate. Despite the best efforts of our family and her doctors, it seemed nothing could get her turned around in the direction of better health. It had been a very dry fall season that year with almost no rain, and it was now December 23rd, the day before Christmas Eve day. Up until that time, there had been a minimal amount of rain, but now heavy rains were suddenly in the forecast. On the evening of the twenty-third, I suddenly thought to myself

"Here we go, things aren't looking good for Mom health wise, and it's going to get much worse." My heart hurt deeply to think those thoughts, but I just knew through Clair cognizance that difficult days were directly ahead for her.

The next day on Christmas Eve day, she started having one small TIA stroke after another, while at the same time it started to torrentially pour down rain. It had been such a dry autumn with sparse rainfall, but now it was coming down in buckets. On Christmas Eve a male in spirit stood beside me. I could feel his presence as he very softly and solemnly communicated a telepathic message to me. He said, "Your Mom will have these strokes for about one week, after which time she will rapidly deteriorate for two months." Then no words were communicated, but instead I was clairvoyantly shown a "flat line."

Listening to the message with much upset and denial, I accepted the fact she might indeed go downhill physically, but I refused to accept the clairvoyant image of the flat line. Of course the flat line referred to a hospital flat line, when there is no longer a heartbeat from the patient. However, I would not accept the fact this clairvoyance meant Mom's heart would stop. Instead, I hoped it simply meant she might linger on with physical life, even though there would be additional bodily weakening. At the time I was in total denial regarding the flat line, but it was the only way I could cope with my emotions, since the thought of loosing her in the physical sense was too difficult to think about.

Spirit had been correct regarding the two telepathic messages a few months earlier in October. A female, my Mother, was indeed starting to make the progression toward Heaven, between the dry autumn season and the wet season of heavy rains. Her strokes did start on that Christmas Eve night, which marked the turning point from the dry fall to the wet California winter.

The fact the message from spirit stated she would start going toward Heaven once again confirmed my understanding of the passing process. When a passing process is gradual; we actually begin to "grow toward Heaven," rather than instantly "go to Heaven" at our last heartbeat. When this process is ongoing rather than instant, it becomes one of gradual transformation from this side to that one. The silver cord is severed at our last heartbeat, which finalizes a separation of the spiritual body from the physical self. But until that time occurs, the passing does become a measured process of crossing over.

In January and February, I started to experience different spiritual events around Mom and the home as Heaven drew closer, and her connection with the spiritual side grew ever stronger. During this time, I experienced a third eye clairvoyance and various other sixth sense happenings, realizing that Heaven was very close at hand for her. The fact these experiences were increasing was proof to me of her extreme closeness to The Other Side.

Not only were my spiritual events increasing in number, but she also began to experience her own sixth sense phenomenon. Several weeks before her passing, I was at her bedside when she suddenly spoke up and said, "I see a man." She was looking several feet directly in front of the bed she was in, intently staring at the empty air. Of course there was no one there in the physical sense and five feet beyond the bed was wall. I hesitantly asked, "What is this man doing?" having no idea what she would say. Her reply was very sincere and earnest as she quickly replied, "He is waiting for me."

When hearing her say that, it hit me very hard as I knew she was being honest, and her spiritual eyes were now being opened. At the time, her physical eyesight was extremely poor, but now her spiritual eyes were starting to see. She spoke no more about the man that was waiting for her, and I asked nothing else about it. It was too hard emotionally for me to discuss it further, so I remained silent.

A few days later she suddenly took a turn for the worse. Her health was now so bad it was only a matter of time until her frail physical body could no longer support life. During this time, I remained in a state of denial continually hoping the flat line that had been clairvoyantly shown to me the previous December would mean she would linger, at least for awhile. Of course this would never happen, but I had to keep hoping for my own emotional sake, and I refused to give up on that hope.

One day during her state of critically poor health, I ran out to the mailbox, quickly grabbing the mail and then hurrying back inside. While rushing to pick up the mail, I saw Heaven directly above the house. It was an entire landscape superimposed right above me filled with many beautiful colors and much vibrant scenery. Normally when seeing Heaven, I will experience some of the magnificence of the place, feeling the wonderful unconditional love that is ever-present there. Although I could see it clairvoyantly, my clairsentience had shut down, with that paranormal sense being numbed because of the very difficult emotional situation. With Heaven appearing on top of the house, I knew the time of her passage must be very close at hand. Clairvoyantly seeing this once again confirmed my belief, that this wonderful place called Heaven is actually right on top of us in a much higher energy dimension than the earth plane.

A couple days before she passed, I was at her bedside when suddenly Dad's face became superimposed directly on hers, with his face appearing much like he looked shortly before he passed numerous years earlier. This type of phenomenon is called transfiguration, when a spirit will superimpose their image over someone else. My feeling is that it was a sign, that Dad wanted to show me the two of them were in the process of being reunited, and he was the man she had seen weeks earlier that was waiting for her.

Those in Heaven can alter their physical appearance much like we put on a different set of clothing, since they no longer have our physical limitations. They can appear as their true thirty year old heavenly selves, or they can show themselves as they appeared while living on Earth. This transfiguration vision lasted for about seven or ten seconds. Then it was gone as quickly as it had appeared, and Mom's face was once again the face of an older person about to pass.

Finally the day of her passing arrived, but at the time, none of us in the family realized the actual day had finally come. Some of my sense awareness had been shut down, since I refused to accept the flat line that had been clairvoyantly shown to me over two months earlier. However, in hindsight, there was a physical telltale sign her crossover had arrived which was not recognized at the time.

Hours before her departure, I was in the neighboring room next to hers and suddenly heard the most beautiful voice coming from her room. Through Clair cognizance, I knew without a doubt it was Mom's voice. She was so very frail and unable to physically talk at the time, but yet I heard her voice with so much depth and incredible beauty. She called out my name very loudly, only saying that one word. The strength and energy of her voice was amazing, and it went far beyond her human capabilities with her extremely poor health.

How could she speak with such a vibrant and clear voice? I do believe it was her heavenly voice filled with great emotion and love that I heard that day. Being so close to passing, I feel she was in both worlds at once and was able to use her soul voice right here on the physical earth plane. Being a clairaudient, I will normally hear those on the spiritual side speaking with thought impression and occasionally speaking telepathically directly into my ear. However, this voice was different than the normal clairaudient voice, because it was originating right here on Earth. Despite the fact it was her heavenly voice, she had indeed managed to channel that voice directly to the fifth sense physical plane.

Mom did crossover at the end of February, going to her heavenly home, and everything had come to pass exactly as it had been foretold by spirit. She did start to go toward Heaven between the dry autumn and wet winter, with the small strokes starting the very night it started to pour down rain. These strokes lasted for about one week, and after that time, there was rapid deterioration for two months, with her last heartbeat coming at that time. Of course the flat line that had been clairvoyantly shown to me did refer to that final heartbeat.

A number of days later during her funeral service, I was sitting in the front row with family feeling very empty and lost, knowing such a heartfelt loved one was gone from the physical plane. During that time, I suddenly had third eye clairvoyance, knowing without a doubt it was totally real and coming in from the higher realms. In my mind's eye, I could see both Mom and Dad. They had been reunited and were once again joined together as kindred loving spirits in Heaven.

While watching the two of them during the clairvoyance, I could see the great joy on their faces and feel the peace in their hearts. They were totally filled with bliss and contentment, delighted at being together once again. Although they had been separated from each other in the physical sense for numerous years, I could sense it felt to them like they had only been apart for a moment. This made perfect sense to me because time on that side is so much different than here on Earth. Since there is no time in Heaven as we know it, life there is simply measured as eternal. Despite the fact they had been away from each other for those numerous years, it made no difference now. Those years of being physically apart had become the proverbial twinkling of an eye to them, now that they were both with each other in their heavenly home.

As they were standing together side by side, I observed Mom and Dad as they looked down on the funeral service. During the entire time while watching the service, they radiated great love and joy to everyone in attendance. They showed no sadness in their faces, but instead exhibited a wonderful caring and affection for everyone there.

One night during sleep months after her passing, Mom instantly appeared to me on the astral plane. I like to think of the astral plane as a spiritual plane of existence where our spirits can go for communication, information, and problem solving. In that place, the spiritual side can communicate to us, hopefully providing us with information and help in our everyday lives. However, there are many levels to this plane of existence from the lower to the very high, so it is always wise to reach out and strive for the very highest levels. This is where purity of truth and helpful assistance can come from.

When seeing her on the astral plane, she appeared vibrant and full of life, displaying a quality of great inner strength. Her face had no wrinkles, and she was totally in the prime of her life. She only spoke three words saying, "Look who's here!" as she beamed with great childlike innocence and enthusiasm. Standing behind her was Dad in his wonderful thirty year old body with the same brown wavy hair he had been blessed with as a young man on Earth.

Although I had seen Mom and Dad on the heaven plane during the funeral service, this was the first time I had seen Dad on the astral plane since Mom's passing. It was a thrilling moment for me, and my spirit immediately broke out with a flood of joyful tears telepathically yelling, "Dad!" Since I was in spirit form having traveled to the astral plane during sleep, the tears were merely a thought form. Even though it was only thought, it was every bit as real as tears in the physical sense, since all thoughts are tangible and real on a spiritual level.

Despite my momentary flood of tears, Dad displayed only one tear in each eye. Although each tear signified extreme joy, I do feel they indicated something in addition to that. Dad was not only joyful, but he was also displaying the fact he now felt totally blessed because his loved one was once again with him. He lowered his head slightly, and through clairsentience, I felt he was showing his respect for my having watched out for her when she was on the earth plane. Before he had passed, his spirit had requested that I help and watch over her, and now he was showing admiration by thanking me with his body language. It was wonderful to see the two of them so happy and full of life. Waking up the next morning, I experienced great inner peace, knowing they are both in Heaven feeling such outstanding eternal bliss.

Six months later, the first Christmas season without her was quickly approaching. Normally the first holidays without a loved one are difficult for most people, and I was no exception. Missing her physical presence during that festive time of year, I sat in a chair solemnly reminiscing the many previous Christmases when she had been with our family. While sitting there I received a message from spirit, simply being told, "Wait until Christmas." After receiving that communication, I started to think about it, wondering what spirit might have meant. Christmas was still over two weeks away, and the message was mystifyingly confusing.

When Christmas drew close, one of my brothers and his wife called saying they wanted to come for a Christmas meal. Since they were unable to come on Christmas Day, they said they would come the day after, and we would have a festive meal at that time. In preparation for the meal, I decided to set the dinner table the evening before their arrival, which happened to be Christmas Day evening.

After getting it set, I was about ten feet away from the table when suddenly an amazing clairvoyance came through. Standing next to the dinner table was Mom displaying all of her heavenly radiance. She was looking down at the place settings on the table with a big smile of approval on her face. Since she had always enjoyed preparing meals for family and friends while on Earth, she was letting me know that everything looked just fine and perfect.

As she stood there, I was unable to tell what she was wearing, because my clairvoyant third eye immediately went to the breathtaking colors emanating from her entire spiritual self. Her heavenly aura displayed a multitude of various beautiful shades that literally pulsated and glowed from her body. Over the years, I have always been awestruck when seeing heavenly loved ones who are momentarily visiting on Earth. The colors they radiate are unlike any colors in the physical sense. Mom was briefly visiting from a place that has an extremely high vibration and energy level, and that energy level was displayed with the warm colors radiating from her. Because of the differential between earth's slower vibration and her faster vibration, it was possible to clairvoyantly witness her with those colorful energies around her.

In the sixth sense world, the senses will sometimes blend together. Because of this, it was possible to not only see the spectacular colors around her, but to also feel them. The energies radiated a feeling of great elation and unconditional love, as I knew she was experiencing perfect contentment and peace. After witnessing her standing by the table for maybe fifteen seconds, she was once again gone. However, the feeling of Heaven around her was so powerful it stayed with me for a long time. For days after her appearance, I continued to sense the wonderful clairvoyance, personally experiencing a portion of her great delight of living in such an elevated plane of existence. It was an occurrence I will always remember.

Spirit had once again given a correct message over two weeks earlier when they told me through clairaudience to "wait until Christmas." Feeling low in spirit at the time from missing her, I had no idea what they meant. However, they knew the great joy that was directly ahead of me on Christmas Day evening as I viewed her heavenly self. Since they can see our past, present, and future; Mom was able to plan the earthly visit on that particular day, knowing I would be setting the dinner table for the meal with family. She had wanted to briefly be with me on Christmas and to give me great happiness. Her brief stopover that evening once again confirmed to me, that she is an extremely healthy and happy individual, in that awe-inspiring place we often refer to as Paradise.

19

The Perfect Friend And Gift

About one year after Mom's passage to heaven, I was standing in my bedroom when her voice suddenly broke through the silence. Many times since her passing, she had spoken to me through thought impression during sleep or when awake, but this time it was different. She spoke telepathically into my right ear, just as if she were standing next to me in the physical sense. This type of communication occurs less frequently for me than telepathic messaging done by thought impression; however this way of speaking directly into the ear does happen at times.

How did I know it was her speaking that afternoon? As long as I know or have known a person that is living or has lived on Earth, I will recognize their spirit's thought impression or clairaudient voice by their essence, the soul of the person speaking. Many times the voice will sound a little different than their earthly voice, but it is the soul of the person that identifies them self. This soul recognition is instantaneous when hearing a familiar spirit in this manner.

Normally a message coming in will be rather brief, being only a shorter sentence in length at the most. However, this time the communication was actually a bit longer as she firmly said, "You will meet a friend. Think of it as a gift from me." That is all she said, and then there was once again silence in the air.

It was very surprising but also fascinating that she would come through in such a strong definitive way. At the time, there seemed to be great importance to the message with her clarity of voice speaking in this direct manner. Immediately, I began thinking about what had been said and who this person might be, contemplating various possibilities of how a new friendship would come about. The message seemed intriguing, but it was also quite baffling. I had always found spirit to speak the truth, and I felt no doubt that in time the answer to this message would come about.

A few weeks later, I was online doing searches on different subjects and looking at various sites on those topics. Suddenly a strong urge came over me to do a search on absent healing. This feeling seemed to be a very strong clairsentient emotion where I was actually being guided and pushed by an unseen force to do that search. Absent healing is a subject that has often fascinated me, and when the clairsentience came through, there was no doubt that a search on this topic should be done.

After doing the search, I looked at various absent healing sites and happened to notice one website in particular that looked intriguing. When looking at these sites, I was actually reading the energies off of each one, looking for a website that had special qualities of lightness and pureness around it. After glancing at a number of them and looking for these characteristics, I found one that met these qualities and was amazed at the wonderful energies coming from it. The energies were very elevated, pure, and wholesome, and they were exactly what I had been searching for.

It was a very interesting website, discussing absent healing and other spiritually related topics. There was a contact address on the home page with a request that people feel free to write to this person if they desired. Feeling a very powerful urge, I sent an email off to the person at that address with subdued anticipation of a possible reply.

Two days later, it was a pleasant surprise when a reply email came back from a woman who called herself Dee. It was a nice friendly email and displayed the same qualities of pureness that I had sensed in her website. When starting to read the correspondence, I was taken by surprise because she began by saying, "Hello my friend." For some unexplainable reason, there was a deep message in those words that touched my heart in a very real way. When reading those three words, it felt like we were already the best of friends, even though I had only written to her one time, and this was her first reply back. It was puzzling why that short phrase struck such a note of harmony within me, but the answer to that feeling would make itself known in the weeks and months to come.

After this first communication, our friendship immediately grew by leaps and bounds. Within a matter of weeks, we had instantly become the best of friends, as our camaraderie seemed to grow stronger with each passing day. I found out that Dee lived in England, a distance of about fifty-four hundred miles from my home in California. Despite the great mileage distance between us, our friendship became so strong, it felt as if we lived right next door to each other.

Through our constant emails back and forth, I discovered that Dee and I had something very significant in common. She told me that she was also an intuitive and had been her entire life, having many psychic experiences similar to mine. As we began to share our paranormal experiences with each other, we found out that we had much more in common than we ever thought had been possible. It was amazing and exciting to share these occurrences, knowing that each of us fully understood what it is like to experience so many different types of sixth sense events.

Dee also told me that she sends out healing, not only to friends and family, but also to people emailing her through her absent healing website. Absent healing is a type of energy channeling and transfer, where the absent healer will be used as a medium, or intermediary, between the high energy realms and the person receiving the healing from those high places. Many times it is done through prayer, since prayer is the great up lifter, providing a direct connection with the high energies and transferring some of those elevated energies to the recipient. Two very important energies from the high realms are the White Light of the Holy Spirit and the God Light. Both can play an important part in the absent healing process, and when properly done, this procedure will give the recipient a feeling of inner peace and uplifted energies.

The fact Dee was sending out healing to people using such pure high vibrations was evident when initially reading the energies off her site. I had been searching for an absent healing website with much pureness, and her site was merely reflecting the energies of her absent healing actions. We do live in a world of energy vibration, with our thoughts and actions creating varying degrees of positivity or negativity around us, including everything we affiliate with. Her work with channeling and sending out positive high realm energies actually became visible to me when looking at her website.

When seeing uplifting energies around something, I will clairvoyantly see goodness and pureness around it, shining like a beacon of light. The reverse is true with negativity, as I will then see darkness and impurity, with a clairsentient feeling of conflict and disharmony.

As additional weeks progressed, it seemed our closeness became inseparable. The more we learned about each other, the more we realized a great and lasting friendship had been made. We had so much in common regarding our spiritual experiences, and we thoroughly enjoyed sharing them with each other.

Bubbling over with excitement at the strong companionship that had been formed, one night during sleep I had the desire to astral travel over to her home in England. Astral traveling is the way our spirits can journey from place to place right here on Earth, or we can even dimension travel to other planes of existence. During sleep, we can move freely while our physical body rests, with both the physical and spiritual bodies always staying attached to each other by the silver cord. It is possible to be in two places at once since we are multidimensional beings, always having both a physical and spiritual side. Dee has often smiled when saying, "Astral travel is not only fast, but it is also very cost efficient and without the normal annoyances of physical travel."

During that particular night while sleeping, I did just that, astral traveling over to England to see my good friend Dee. During that time of year there was an eight hour time difference between California and England, so as my physical body slept during the night in California, my spiritual body made the trip over to England where it was daytime. Never having been to her house in the physical sense how did my spiritual self know where to go? It is hard for us to consciously understand, but in spirit form we just "know," and there is never any need to look at a map or ask for directions. Our spiritual side simply thinks of a place to go and we are there in an instant.

As my physical self slept, instantly I found my spiritual body floating a couple of feet above the floor in her house. Since I was in spirit form, there was no need to stand on the floor unless wanting to, so it was perfectly ok and normal to hover if desired. Through Clair cognizance, I immediately knew it was the kitchen in her home and also noticed Dee standing by the kitchen counter. I was totally ecstatic to be with her, and even though she was in physical form at the counter and I was in spiritual form, it made no difference. We were together and that made our friendship bond seem even stronger.

While hovering in the corner of the kitchen looking over at her, I noticed she became aware of me and could sense my presence. Raising my arms, I stretched both arms and hands out toward her, telepathically saying, "God bless you." While saying that, I instantly observed beautiful colors of energies coming out from my fingertips traveling directly to her. There were all the colors of the rainbow in stunningly vibrant shades that were being sent through the fingers as I channeled these elevated energies from the high realms to her. I was acting as an intermediary between Dee and the high dimensions, giving her a blessing from God.

After she had received the blessing, I was suddenly gone from the room. In hindsight, it was apparent I had astral traveled to her home, not only to be with her for a few joyful moments, but also to give her a very special blessing from above.

Later discussing the incident with Dee, she told me that she had indeed sensed my presence in the kitchen that day and had in fact said, "Hello John." I knew at the time she could sense me as her head turned slightly in my direction, and she became motionless for a brief second or two. She was deep in thought, and I could sense her thoughts were on me being in the kitchen. Interestingly, I didn't hear her say, "Hello John," but I could tell she knew my spiritual side was there with her.

When acting as an intermediary to channel the blessing to her, I placed my thoughts on the high energies of the God Light and The Other Side, instantly making the connection with those energies. Once the connection had been made, it was possible to channel them through my fingertips directly to her. Energies play a major significance on the spiritual side and can actually be seen by people using clairvoyance. Since the spiritual energies can vary from low to high, it is always important to place our thoughts on the high energies of light. It is those vibrations that are composed of everything pure and good, and because of that purity, will give off and radiate the breathtaking colors.

What an amazing gift Mom had given me, when a few weeks before meeting Dee online, she had said through clairaudience, "You will meet a friend. Think of it as a gift from me." She had found someone that would become an enduring friend, and even though Dee and I were on two separate continents, she found a way to bring the two of us together.

How was she able to locate a person so far away and yet so similar to me in so many ways? That is one of the fascinating aspects of those in Heaven, as they do have knowledge and wisdom that goes beyond our understanding. Although that wisdom is limited for those residing there, it still far exceeds anything we have here on Earth. Everything in Heaven expands in a greater way. The colors are infinitely more colorful, the joy is much more uplifting, and all the senses and wisdom are greatly magnified.

However it became possible for Mom to find Dee and bring the two of us together, I will forever remain grateful for her very generous gift. It seems she did the nearly impossible, finding that special person that would fit perfectly into my life. For that reason, I will always thank her, knowing that she did find the perfect friend and gave me the most perfect gift.

20

Ghost Girl Needing Help

As additional months passed, Dee and I continued to strengthen our newly found relationship. We were having an enjoyable and rewarding time discussing our sixth sense experiences, comparing the similarities and parallels between her occurrences and mine. It was fascinating to find a person that had so much in common with me, and the fact we both experienced so many paranormal events in our lives became the primary link for our strong connection.

The bond between the two of us became so strong we began sharing similar experiences during sleep, meeting up on the astral plane or taking an astral trip to each other's home on the earth plane. As we slept, it became possible for each of us to make these trips in spiritual form away from our physical body, returning to our physical self afterwards. When going to the astral plane, we can meet up with people or go there to do analysis and problem solving regarding events in our lives. Should we decide to stay right on the physical plane, we can also make an astral trip to a place on Earth.

Since there is no time as we know it on the astral plane, it becomes possible for the two of us to meet and experience the same event, even though we are sleeping at different hours. Most of the year there is an eight hour time difference between England and California.

Interestingly, our similar experiences are usually on the same night, except for our different sleeping times due to the eight hour time difference. It is hard to comprehend planes of existence where time is different than Earth since we are used to a past, present, and future. But when astral traveling to other planes such as the astral and heaven planes, there is an eternal quality where time seems to stand still, and everything is simply measured in the moment and by the event.

One night during sleep, I stayed on the earth plane, taking an astral trip over to see Dee in England. As my spiritual self ventured over to her home, I was met with much hospitality and warmth. Her spiritual side greeted me with the affection and kindness of a long time friend, even though we hadn't known each other for that many months.

Even though Dee's spiritual side met me with warmth and kindness, I did feel a small amount of nervousness during the first two astral trips, due to the fact I wanted to make a good impression. Feeling a bit reserved and formal during our first couple of meetings, I was polite but also a bit shy. In addition to the newness of our friendship, the energies of England were very much different than the energies of California, making me very aware I was in a place far from home. The energies of that country were very pleasant, but they were of course very dissimilar from those of my own locale.

Because I wanted to make a nice impression along with sensing the energies of a different country, my demeanor was a bit reserved during the first few astral trips to her home. However, after the first few visits, I started to feel much more relaxed, no longer feeling the need to be as reserved and timidly polite. Dee was an amazing person filled with much gentleness and compassion, with those wonderful qualities then making me feel very comfortable.

On another particular night during sleep, I was again with Dee in England. It was daytime for her, and I found her expecting me, once more greeting me with enthusiasm and open arms. Unlike the astral visit when she was working in the physical sense in the kitchen as I hovered sending her God's blessing, this time it was her spirit that was waiting for me. Her spiritual side had been expecting me, and there seemed to be a reason for our getting together. Both of us were in spiritual form, but it seemed perfectly normal for us, and we conversed through telepathy just as if we were in our physical bodies talking in the normal physical manner. We seemed to chat for quite a while, enjoying each other's company with big smiles on our faces. Both of us were so grateful to be together again, totally enjoying every moment of the reunion.

At the time, Dee lived in a two story home, with the living quarters on the first floor and the bedrooms upstairs. That is typical of England, since many homes have at least two floors. Both of us were on the bottom floor having a nice friendly chat when suddenly I heard a voice coming from the upstairs. It was a tiny soft voice that was barely audible and recognizable. The quiet voice said, "Help me!" and then once again repeated those words. After listening, I realized it was the voice of a young girl, possibly around seven or eight years old. She spoke so faintly it was difficult to hear her, but the gentle and innocent tone when she spoke made me instantly realize she was quite young.

Immediately I asked, "Did you hear that?" Dee looked at me with a bit of puzzlement on her face, as if she hadn't heard the barely audible voice. I then said, "It seems to be coming from upstairs. Let's go see who it is." As we started walking up the flight of stairs, I could feel every step underfoot. In spirit form, it is possible to hover in the air or pass through walls and solid objects since we no longer have physical limitations. But it is also possible to act as if we are still in physical form, walking on floors and going up steps. For whatever reason, our spiritual selves were using the physical way of walking with the feel of the stairs under our feet.

While going to the upper floor, we continued to hear the soft cries of help from the little child. After entering Dee's bedroom, I noticed the girl's voice was coming from behind a small door. Later after this experience, I found out there was indeed a small door in her bedroom which led to the attic. Up to this point, I had never seen a physical photo of her bedroom and had no idea there was an access door to the attic in that location.

Standing in her bedroom by the door to the attic area, it felt like Dee and I then walked right through the door never having opened it, which is totally possible in spirit form. Looking around the dark space, I suddenly spoke to Dee and excitedly said, "There she is." She was standing in one corner of the attic space, and I sensed she felt very confused and alone. The energies of her aura were quite dark, so it was difficult to see her in the darkened attic. However, after locating her, we were both delighted with full-sized smiles on our faces that she had been found.

She was a little ghost girl, puzzled and at a loss, waiting for someone to come and help her. Ghosts live in their own dimension, stuck in a place and time unable to move on to The Light of The Other Side. It is possible for many people that normally do not have paranormal experiences to see ghosts, since the dimension they exist in is actually very close in energy to the earth plane. For that reason, ghosts are closer to physical manifestation and are sometimes able to be more easily seen than those in true spirit form on The Other Side.

Under normal circumstances, a ghost will simply reject to go home to The Light and will insist on staying close to Earth. Although they are no longer alive in the physical sense, they still continue to have a strong tie to the earth plane, which keeps them earthbound. They can be quite stubborn regarding their situation, refusing to move on because of the earthly attachment they refuse to give up. However, in the case of ghost children, I feel most are simply confused about their passing and need some help in crossing over to the higher realms of The Other Side. Many children will see a footbridge to cross over, and in rare instances that footbridge might be confusing for them, so therefore they refuse to go over it. Most do not exist in ghost form out of stubbornness, but rather out of innocence and confusion.

I wholeheartedly believe that God will always send some type of help for these children that feel perplexed about their passing. He will not allow them to exist in that dimension, because they are there out of innocence, not out of tenacity and obstinacy. They want to move forward to The Light of The Other Side, being reunited with their passed over friends and loved ones, but they just don't know how to get there.

Immediately after locating the little girl, Dee and I started to spiritually go to work channeling the brilliant energies of light to the child. I remember stretching our arms and hands out toward the girl, and instantly the darkened attic filled with the breathtaking colors of the higher realms that were being channeled to her. These outstanding energies were going from our fingertips moving directly to the child. While seeing these colors traveling through the air over to her, I felt very awed and humbled to once again witness the incredible beauty of these high energies. Dee and I were being used as intermediaries to channel them to the girl, acting as the mediums between Heaven and the child. Once The Light had been channeled to her, she could then make the instant connection with the higher realms, allowing her to move on to The Other Side.

That is the last remembrance I have about the experience of channeling light to the girl and the trip over to see Dee. Instantly, my spiritual self was joined with my physical body, and I was back in the bedroom asleep in California, fifty-four hundred miles away from England and the attic in her home.

After awakening the next morning and thinking about the occurrence, it became obvious that the astral trip to England during the night had a definite purpose. Although it was a lot of fun to once again see Dee, the purpose of the trip wasn't about meeting and chatting with her. Rather, it was about helping a little child that was stuck in a dimension where she didn't belong. The little ghost girl was in a plane of existence very foreign to her, and she was clearly asking for help. I do feel God placed her in that attic so both Dee and I, being in spiritual form, could locate her and come to her rescue by channeling The Light to her. While asleep during the night in California, my spirit had sensed the call for help with my spiritual self quickly making the astral trip over to England.

The following day after that experience, I sent Dee an email to discuss it. In the email, I described various furnishings in her bedroom, right down to the antique wooden chair close the attic access door. She replied that the description of her room was totally correct, even though I had never previously seen a photo of the room. Having been there in spirit form, I clearly remembered a variety of features in the bedroom.

Although the young girl had a great desire to leave the ghost dimension and go home to The Other Side, most adult ghosts have a stubborn refusal to move on. They have had some type of situation during their life on Earth that has created a very strong tie for them to the earth plane. The tie they feel never seems to be about money or material possessions except for possibly land, since those things are immaterial and trivial after leaving Earth. A ghost can feel an earthbound attachment for a person or situation, which is due to unresolved emotion within them, as a result keeping them strongly connected to Earth. The one exception to a material possession is land, and a ghost can feel strong attachment to a piece of soil, wanting to stay on it and not wanting to leave it.

There is an additional problem that most ghosts share. Since the ghost dimension is so closely tied to Earth; most ghosts have no idea they are no longer alive on the earth plane. They feel totally alive and as far as they are concerned, they still very much exist on Earth. However, they will notice that people constantly seem to ignore them, acting as if they aren't even there and don't exist. Some ghosts learn to live with that situation, living harmoniously side by side with humans. Yet others will feel very infuriated and upset that they are constantly disregarded and overlooked by people. This feeling of upset will create even more disharmony for the ghost, making it additionally harder to crossover to The Light.

A simple heartfelt prayer or positive thought directed with pure intention is always the great energy up lifter. Even though a ghost is locked into that dimension out of pure unwillingness to leave, it is possible for a person in that realm to feel prayers and positive thought being offered to them. A ghost does have free will and they will have to decide for them self if it is time to leave that dimension, but these positive energies sent to them can actually help to change the energy field around them. As the aura around them begins to very slowly change, it is entirely possible they will loose their obstinacy and make the decision to move towards The Light. However, it is always their choice to make the crossover, and all we can do is send them the uplifting energies of prayer and positive thought.

The little ghost girl that was in Dee's attic that particular day is a perfect example of desire and intent. She had a great desire and strong yearning to depart from the ghost dimension and go to The Light. With her little cries for assistance making it obvious she wanted to move on, that desire allowed the high energies to be channeled to her, allowing her to have the crossover connection. God would never allow her to exist in a place that she didn't want to be in, and now she is in the prime of her life, experiencing perfect bliss and happiness in that breathtaking dimension known as The Other Side.

21

Spirit Communicates

There are numerous ways spirit can communicate to each of us as we go about our daily living. Those in the higher realms of The Other Side and even our individual spiritual self want very much to be a part of our physical life, giving us help, advice, and even warning when necessary. I have never found a message from spirit to be unimportant, having them communicate to us simply for the sake of casual conversation. Rather, they will always send messages for a specific reason, whenever there is a definite point they want to convey regarding a situation or event in our life. Even if the message may seem trivial and unimportant at the time, there is still a strong motive and distinct purpose why it is being given.

These messages can occur during both waking and sleeping hours, being sent to us through a variety of methods. Some forms such as nighttime astral trips uniting with loved ones, sensing with one or more of our sixth senses, and even the use of electronic equipment such as phones are often used. Many times communications can be very clear-cut and immediately understood, while at other times they seem a lot like riddles, only to be answered and solved at a later date. However, whenever a particular message is received, there is always a reason it has been sent.

One day about a year after Mom had crossed over and gone to Heaven, I came home from a dental appointment and noticed there was a message on the phone. Since there had been no phone message before going to the dentist; I knew it had come in during the scheduled appointment. Standing by the phone, I retrieved the message and started to listen, feeling slightly curious who had called while I was away from home. The phone speaker was turned down at the time, although it was still possible to make out the voices of a male and female talking to each other. My thoughts were more on the dental visit I had just been at, rather than the message on the phone. Because of this, I nonchalantly turned up the speaker volume to listen a second time, thinking it was possibly a phone solicitation or an unimportant call.

What happened next totally astounded and surprised me. After turning up the volume and listening a second time to the message, I couldn't believe what I was hearing. In fact it was so amazing; I had to listen to it numerous times after that. The man speaking on the phone message was me, while the woman speaking was Mom. It was so remarkable and startling to listen to, at first it seemed very difficult to grasp the idea that it was the two of us speaking.

How could this be occurring over the phone? I was familiar and had received phone messages from spirit before, but never had I heard my own voice also giving a message. The communication began with my voice saying in a very matter of fact way "It's just me." While saying that, my vocal modulations seemed to be very firm and definite about that fact. Immediately after that, Mom spoke on the phone message with her voice, sounding exactly as it had been during her later years of life on Earth. It was clearly an older sounding voice, and with the vocal tone and inflection, it was unmistakably hers. She quickly said, "Just you?" with a big question in her voice. I had sounded so firm in the fact it was just me, while she raised a question about that statement, as if it might not be true.

Finally the message ended when I said, "Just me," once again with a definitive and firm tone to my voice.

While listening over and over to the message, I tried to understand and figure out why that had happened. What was the meaning of the phone message and why was it given at that time? It had been around a year since Mom had passed over to The Other Side, and now I was hearing not only her voice, but also my voice as well coming across a piece of electronic equipment. It was truly mindboggling to listen to and fascinating to think about.

We are spiritual beings that inhabit a physical body here on Earth. Unlike The Other Side where we are a spirit having a body, here we are a body having a spirit. Our spiritual side can temporarily leave our physical self and venture to places on Earth or other dimensions, even though we are still very much here in the physical sense. Because of our ability to do that, we are multidimensional beings, but many times our conscious mind in our physical body will block out the fact that we have indeed traveled away from the physical self.

Since one of the means of communication from spirit can be through electronic equipment such as telephones, televisions, and computers, I feel my spiritual side had gone to a higher realm and reunited with Mom. In that dimension both of us sent an important message back to Earth, using the phone and phone answering system as the tools to convey the message. There was no conscious recollection of having done that, but it was obvious that my higher self, along Mom already in spirit, had given the message for a specific reason.

As the weeks passed after this amazing occurrence, I slowly forgot about it, never having figured out exactly what the message had meant. Since many communications from spirit can be like riddles just waiting to be solved, I knew in time the answer to the puzzle would come.

A few months after the mysterious phone message, a friend called that I hadn't seen in a long time. He and his wife were going to be in the area and said they would stop by to say hello. When they arrived, I quickly went to the front door ready to greet them with a friendly smile and warm welcome. He knew that Mom had been very sick before she passed over, and that I had taken care of her during her last year, but strangely he momentarily forgot she was no longer here on the earth plane. After opening the door, he promptly said, "We just wanted to say hi to you and your Mother."

A startled emotion quickly swept over me when he said that. But immediately after that comment, he remembered she was no longer here in the physical sense and hurriedly said, "It's just you." The moment he spoke those words, I had instant recall of the unexplained message that had been left on the answering machine months earlier. It was the message of my firmly stating, "It's just me," while she replied to the statement with a question, but I once again spoke back to her saying, "Just me."

At once after he spoke those words, I instantly knew the meaning of the unsolved phone message. Although Mom was no longer here physically, that made no difference. The phone message was a reminder from Mom and my higher self that she is still very much a part of our family here on Earth. Although she is no longer here on the physical earth plane, she does watch over her cherished loved ones from Heaven. From time to time, her spirit does come down to the Earth plane, and she does come around those that she loves.

What an astonishing phone message from spirit that turned out to be. For a few months it remained an unsolved mystery, but the answer was revealed with great uplifting understanding, that the emotion of love carries very high energies. Those elevated energies connect us on the earth plane with those we treasure that have passed over. They will never forget us, because we are bound and joined to them by the energy force of unconditional love.

Another way spirit can communicate to us is through a vision. Visions can occur for a variety of reasons, but just like other forms of spirit communication, there is always a clear-cut purpose why it is occurring. I view the vision as one type of clairvoyance, where the use of sixth sense clear sight is employed using the physical eyes.

Over the years, I have experienced another type of clairvoyant sight when the eyes are either opened or closed, which involves the third eye chakra. With open or closed eyes, a mental picture will appear using the mind's third eye, which is located between and slightly above the eyebrows. When viewing clairvoyance in this way, it is similar to mentally watching a snapshot, slideshow, or movie. However, the open eye clairvoyance is not being seen with physical eyes, but rather the mental third eye.

A vision for me differs from the mental third eye clairvoyance in that it is seen instead through the physical eyes. When this happens, the vision is a paranormal experience, being viewed directly in a physical way through normal eyesight. It is coming in from a realm beyond the normal five senses, but many times will appear so real, it becomes difficult to differentiate between the vision and normal physical perception. After a vision occurs, I will analyze it, seeing if it was logically possible that it was mere physical eyesight. If it was not rationally possible in a physical fifth sense way, then I will know it was indeed a sixth sense vision.

One evening, I had to go to the local store for a necessary item. Since it was still late winter with the weather being damp and cool, there was some reluctance to go out and get the item. However, it was a required purchase, so I hesitantly got into the car and started to head for the store. One block from the destination while stopped at an intersection and waiting for the stoplight to turn green, I noticed the car in front of me was starting to back up toward my car.

Immediately, a clairsentient feeling of entrapment swept over my entire body. The car directly in front of mine was coming toward me, and the only option was to quickly move my car into reverse. Looking in the rear view mirror to see if it was possible to back up, I then saw the car directly behind me also starting to crowd toward me. When seeing both autos directly in front and behind me coming toward my car, the sensation of being blocked in grew even stronger.

Thoughts of why this was occurring quickly surged through my mind, with a very strong clairsentient feeling of danger being ever-present. Suddenly the stoplight turned green, and the car in front of me quickly started to move forward. As he proceeded further through the intersection, I rapidly followed close behind, wanting to quickly get away from that feeling of danger as fast as possible. While moving through the intersection, a great feeling of freedom came over me. I had escaped peril and was feeling very relieved.

Moments after this incident and while proceeding through the intersection, my thoughts were very confused, as I began to wonder why that had happened. How was it logically possible to have both cars coming toward mine while experiencing such a powerful sixth sense feeling of danger? Was the experience something that had happened in the physical fifth sense way, or was it a sixth sense vision? As I started to question what had just happened, the entrance to the store parking lot quickly approached. After turning into the entrance, it was necessary to make a hard left to get into the narrow parking area. It was a very tight area, with only one row of parking spaces on one side of the drive through lane, with the building mere feet away on the other side.

While proceeding through that area looking for an empty stall, I noticed a car ahead and to the left of mine starting to pull out of a parking space. However, within seconds it was clear something was very wrong with that driver. He would try to rapidly go back in reverse only to once again go forward into the stall. Immediately, a strong clairsentient feeling of danger came over me, the very same feeling that had been experienced a few minutes earlier at the red stoplight.

Once again sensing some type of peril, I instantly stopped my car and proceeded no further. There was a car in the driving lane a little distance ahead of mine and another directly behind. If I pulled forward, I would be blocked in the driving lane and would be in the direct path of the erratic driver trying to leave his parking space. So the best thing to do was to keep the car motionless and stay out of danger, keeping away from that driver.

While watching this male driver, it became obvious he was most likely intoxicated. In fact, observing his driving ability, it appeared he was extremely inebriated and totally lacked the skills to back out of that space. He repeatedly attempted to back out only to once again go forward into the stall. Finally the car that had been a short distance ahead of mine in the driving lane had pulled forward, so when the intoxicated driver once again pulled out and then proceeded forward into the space; I hurriedly drove my car ahead, going past him and escaping that danger zone.

Once my car was past the location where his car could hit mine, I was able to find a place to park and go inside the store, alerting the manager of the problem. The unpredictable driver's car had hit the car in the adjacent parking space, and the situation needed to be reported. What had started out as a normal short trip over to the store turned out to be a paranormal experience with a warning from spirit. In hindsight, I realized the incident at the stoplight had been a vision forewarning me of the danger that was two minutes ahead in the store parking lot.

The feeling of hazard while trapped between the two cars at the stoplight was played out a second time after entering that parking area. If it hadn't been for the vision and precognitive feeling of danger at the stoplight, I most likely would not have sensed the ominous situation when approaching the intoxicated driver at the store. Without sensing danger, I would have driven and been forced to stop directly behind that driver trying to leave the parking stall. Spirit had come to my aid that evening, guiding and keeping me from harm. Without the advanced warning and vision sent by those in spirit, the outcome driving into the lot that evening might have been entirely different.

These are two of the many ways spirit can speak directly to us. The first communication was to remind me that although Mom is not here in the physical sense, she is still here spiritually, with her spirit and my higher spiritual self reminding me of that fact in the phone message. Our loved ones that have passed over often come around us, and they will always watch over us. They care deeply about our lives here on Earth, continually wanting to give their support and guidance to us.

The second communication by spirit was a vision and clairsentient feeling of danger to forewarn of the impending peril in the parking lot that evening. Once again, it shows how those on The Other Side care for our welfare and want to help whenever possible. There are many in the high realms that want to be here for us, and they include loved ones, angels, and God. When we place our thoughts on the high energies of those realms, it creates an instant connection between those high places and us. That connection can be strengthened the more we concentrate on those energies. All we have to do is ask for their help and direction, and they will hear us.

22

Someone At The Door

The deep friendship and powerful spiritual connection Dee and I share is truly amazing. She became an instant friend for life a few weeks after my passed over Mom spoke directly into my ear, saying I would meet a friend and to think of it as a gift from her. At the time, I was thinking it would be a new friend in my own surrounding area. Little did I realize that this friend she was giving me would turn out to live in England, well over five thousand miles from California.

Meeting on the internet, we immediately felt an unusually close connection with each other. In fact Dee's first email reply to my initial email started with a cheerful and sincere "Hello my friend." When reading those first words in the correspondence, it was as if she already knew we would become the closest of friends. A lifelong intuitive, sensitive, and psychic like me, she must have instantly sensed the deep bond and connection we would share in the future. Those three words that had been written in her first email touched my heart with great resonance and meaning. A very special and incredible amity was about to start for each of us, and I could feel it after reading those short three words.

It is truly fascinating and remarkable that Mom could

find such a special friend. Despite the distance in miles, our connection flourished from the very start of our newly found relationship. Within months we were able to meet up on the astral plane, working jointly and channeling light to a specific problem or person in need of some assistance. We would also astral travel back and forth to each others' homes just for the fun of our spiritual selves getting together and having a visit, or once again channeling light from The Other Side to a specific situation.

It is also possible for us to sense how each other is feeling without an email or phone call. By simply tuning into Dee's energies and vibration level, I will immediately know what type of day or night she is having, and she does the same with me. The energies off our sent emails will constantly change depending upon the way we are feeling at the moment and in present time. Our connection is very "real time," and when tuning in, we will know how each other is at that very moment.

One time during the start of our relationship, Dee sent me a friendship card which was very slow in coming through the mail. It was taking way too long to receive, and we were wondering if it would even arrive from England. She would write an email explaining that it should have arrived, but for some reason there was a big delay. I was feeling a bit nervous about not having received it and was anxiously awaiting its arrival. Our friendship at the time was still quite newly founded, and it seemed I needed to receive that card. I knew in my heart there was no doubt of the special bond that had been formed between us, but I also very much wanted to receive the card from her.

One morning while still in bed, I unexpectedly heard the doorbell ring. It was coming from my front door, but oddly it had a different ring than the normal one. My doorbell tone is longer and plays a short medley of notes, but this ring just went "ding-dong," which certainly was not logical in a fifth sense way.

Although this was mysterious and totally illogical in the physical sense, I didn't recognize that fact at the time. I simply knew that there was someone at the door, and I needed to answer it. Rather than physically get up to answer the door, I automatically let my spiritual self go instead. Why it was done this way would become obvious after the experience. The "ding-dong" of the doorbell once again rang, and through Clair cognizance, or clear knowing, I knew it was obvious that whoever was at the door had an important message to give.

Since our spiritual side has none of the physical limitations of our physical self, we can hover in the air and see through walls, doing these things without any forethought. We are in spirit form after leaving our physical body, having the wonderful freedom of no physical boundaries and restrictions. Of course during our life here, our astral side is always connected to our physical self by the silver cord, and they will always stay attached until it is time to physically leave the earth plane.

As my spiritual body glided through the living room and then hovered toward the front door, I glanced through the wall of the house to see who it was. Much to my delight I viewed three males in spirit standing directly outside the door. As they patiently waited, each had a warm glowing smile and childlike innocence on their face. Rather than hover in mid air, they were standing on the ground, and I could tell by their demeanor they had come down to the earth plane from The Other Side. Each of these eternal looking thirty year olds had the unconditionally pure energies of the high realms around them. Filled with those wonderful energies, they happily stood there enjoying every moment of their momentary trip away from Heaven.

As I hovered in the living room watching them through the wall, they suddenly communicated a telepathic message. There was no need to physically answer the door since I was in spirit form and would not have been able to physically open it. They knew through Clair cognizance I had seen them, and that I was viewing them through the house wall. The message they gave was brief, which is normal when receiving a communication from spirit. I am not sure which one of the three males sent this telepathic message, but that made no difference. The important thing is that the communication had been received by me, and they had done the job they were sent to do.

Through thought transference, one of them said, "You will receive a card from Dee." It was such a short message, but it brought me much peace of mind knowing that a card from her would indeed arrive. After hearing that message, instantly I found my astral self back in the bed reunited with my physical body. The ecstatically joyful thirty year old males from Heaven had vanished as quickly as they had appeared at my door. I felt very appreciative to think they would take the time to come and give that meaningful message.

The same day after receiving the morning message from spirit, I went to the mailbox and was pleased to see that a card from Dee had arrived. Spirit was not only correct in saying it would arrive, but they decided to tell me the very morning before it came. What a thoughtful and kind gesture it was of them to have delivered that gratifying message.

The next morning I wrote Dee telling her the card had arrived. Much to my surprise, she replied by saying she had asked spirit to remind me that it was on its way, asking them that it be delivered as soon as possible. Looking back upon that event, I then understood that the different sounding tone of the doorbell that morning made no difference when hearing it. Since thoughts are things in the spiritual world, those three men were simply conveying the thought of a ringing doorbell, which I then heard with clairaudient ears. That would also explain why my spiritual self automatically went toward the door rather than getting out of bed in the physical sense. When hearing the "ding-dong," my spiritual side instantly knew it was being heard through a psychic sense, and it was not a fifth sense event. We can be so thankful that we have those from the high realms, who are gladly willing to help out in any way they can and whenever possible. They want to be here for us, and all we have to do is ask for their help.

On another occasion, Dee was expecting a parcel to arrive at her home. After looking up the tracking information, she realized it would be most likely arrive the following day. She did have some errands to do away from the house on the day of delivery, but she knew the delivery person would leave a note on the door saying they had been there if she weren't home. If she happened to be out of the house when the person came, she would just phone up the company and have it delivered the next business day.

Not thinking anymore about the expected delivery the next day in England, I went off to bed and awoke feeling startled at what occurred at 4:45 a.m. In a deep sleep, I was abruptly awakened at that time with the sound of knocking at my front door. During that time of year, it was still completely dark outside that early in the morning. Coming out of a deep sleep, the knocking totally surprised and confused me, as I curiously listened to a total of six raps. Each rap was fast and definite, with all six taking only a couple of seconds to complete. Feeling stunned and perplexed that someone would be at my door so early in the morning, I tried to fully awaken and make the decision whether or not to answer it. With it still completely dark outside, it seemed very odd that someone would be knocking at that time of morning.

Still lying in bed, I made the decision to see if the person at the door would repeat the raps. If it was extremely urgent, I figured they would most likely knock again, and then I would get up to see who it was. By this time, I was almost fully roused from the deep slumber, but I continued to stay quiet and motionless in bed, waiting to hear if additional raps would come. While listening and waiting for more knocks, the only thing that could be heard was the perfect quiet of the early morning. There was complete silence in the house and after intently listening for a minute; I started to relax, releasing the anticipation of hearing additional knocking.

By this time, I was fully awakened and while still lying in bed, started to wonder what had just occurred. Had there been someone at my door at such an odd hour of the morning? Within about a minute of thinking about the situation, the thought suddenly went through my mind that it wasn't my door, but rather a person at Dee's door that I had heard. A Clair cognizant sense of knowing told me that for some reason, I had just heard someone knocking at my friend's door in England fifty-four hundred miles away. Feeling very content at having solved the mysterious door rapping, I quickly turned over in bed, drifting back off into a relaxing sleep for a few more hours.

The following day, I sent Dee an email explaining what had happened, telling her of the uncharacteristic door tapping at four forty-five in the morning. I explained to her there were a total of six knocks, with each one being very loud and distinct. When she replied back, she told me that her expected parcel had arrived at exactly twelve forty-five England time. She was unable to be at home during the delivery, but he did leave a note on the door saying he had tried to deliver the package, and that he had dated the note as 12:45 p.m.

During that time of year, there is an eight hour time difference between England and California. When reading her reply email, it was positively confirmed to me that I had indeed heard her door rapping. The knocking at my front door that morning abruptly awoke me from a deep sleep, making me at first think it was a fifth sense event, and there was actually someone at my door in physical form.

Exactly what happened that early morning, and why would the knocking be so loud and distinct, causing me to instantly awaken from a deep sleep? Although at first I thought it was fifth sense and happening in a very physical manner, within minutes it became evident through Clair cognizance it was someone at Dee's door. When the man knocked at her door, I do feel my spiritual side was actually inside Dee's home. Often finding a desire to venture away from the physical body during sleep, I had once again traveled in spirit form, going to a different local, wanting to visit my friend's home in England.

Sometimes there is a separation of awareness between the soul mind and physical consciousness. I had spiritually traveled over to her home, but remained consciously unaware of having done that. When the delivery person knocked at her door, I heard the rapping with my spiritual ears, but with the silver cord connection to my physical self, I also heard it in a fifth sense way as if it were happening at my door. Hearing it in this way caused to me to awaken from the sound sleep. This is very similar to a sixth sense vision that occurs through the physical fifth sense eyes. Hearing the knock that early morning was an extra perceptive event, but I still heard it with my physical ears, just as if it were occurring on the physical plane and at my own door in California.

There is always the connection between our physical and spiritual sides, however weak or strong it may be. When the three males in spirit form came to my door to announce that Dee's card would be arriving soon, it was my spiritual side that saw them. Both the men and I were in spirit form, and they gave their message to me on that level. However, when I physically heard with my ears the delivery person knocking at Dee's door, it was a situation of experiencing a paranormal event on a physical level. The fact I could hear it with the physical ears meant the psychic event was coming through in a fifth sense way.

We are always multidimensional beings, and we are capable of experiencing many types of perception beyond our normal five senses. The universe is full of amazing extra sensory awareness beyond the physical plane. We owe it to ourselves to reach out to the highest possible energies, developing our innate abilities, and becoming the best in tune and perceptive individuals we can possibly be.

23

Connecting With The Light

There is a term I use to describe the method of tuning in and connecting our body, mind, and spirit with the perfect energies of light from the high realms. I call this phrase "Connecting with The Light." It is a process of our reaching out, creating an increasingly powerful link between this side and that one. When we go through this process, we are actually strengthening and magnifying our own energies, creating a happier and more contented self.

Each of us has a natural God given tie between this side and that one, but many times during our life this connection can become fragile and weakened. The hard and trying experiences of life that we often encounter can stifle our spirit and weaken this natural bond. At times we can feel so bogged down with everyday problems, it seems almost impossible to reach out and grab a hold of that special connection that is inherently ours for the taking.

We do come to Earth to experience and hopefully overcome negativity, since Earth is a combination of both the positive and negative. Unlike the perfectly positive energies of The Other Side, here we have a combination of energies ranging from lower to higher. Because of these differing energy levels, Earth is much denser and has a much slower rate of vibration than the energies of the high realms. We do come here to experience all of this, and there is a very important reason why we are here. The difficulties experienced during our earth life create the potential for a great deal of soul growth. It is important that we face our earth challenges head on, working with them the best we can, trying to turn any negative situation into a positive outcome. By doing this we are actually furthering our soul development, which is all done for the glory of God. For that reason Earth becomes the ideal classroom, a place to experience, to learn, and to grow. Our soul, the seat of our spirit, will further nurture and develop when we overcome our challenges and difficulties in the best possible way.

One extremely supportive technique that makes our earth challenges easier is to make as strong a connection as possible with the high vibrations of light. When strengthening that tie, we are allowing the wonderful energies of The Other Side to envelope our life and our decision making, as we go about handling everyday challenges and problems. With the influence of these magnificent energies surrounding us, it makes our life here on Earth easier. We can feel the positive effects of these energies, and they will help direct and guide each of us to live the best possible life we possibly can.

Not only are the incredible energies of Heaven perfect in every way, but the senses there are also infinitely magnified compared to the senses here on Earth. The reason for the great awareness in that breathtaking place is due to the perfect energies that eternally exist in that dimension. God's light shines brilliantly there and everything in that glorious place reflects the perfect energy of His love.

When we start to tune into those energies and they connect with us, it becomes possible for us to experience a small portion of the awareness that is experienced by those in the high realms. When this occurs, our perceptions will go beyond the normal five senses found here on Earth, and we will open up to extra sensory sixth sense perception. We will "see" things not viewed with mere physical eyes, "hear" words and thoughts that are not heard by the normal ear, at times physically or emotionally "feel" something, suddenly have a sense of "knowing", and even "smell" fragrances or "taste" foods not found on Earth. All of these paranormal abilities can be felt when we are properly connected to The Light. It is not a game, but rather a lifelong quest to experience these uplifting and glorious energies; to experience a small portion of the great feeling of perfect positivity that exists there.

As many of you already know, our body here on Earth has seven major energy centers known as chakras. These spinning wheels of light are located from the base of the spine to the top of the head. The seven major chakras are the:

> Bare or Root Chakra, located at the base of the spine
> Sacral Chakra, found in the lower abdomen
> Solar Plexus Chakra, in the solar plexus region
> Heart Chakra, located close to the heart
> Throat Chakra, in the throat region
> Third Eye Chakra, located at the center of the forehead, and the
> Crown Chakra, found at the top of the head

Each of these chakras is designated with a different color, and each has a separate function within the body. When all seven are aligned and balanced, they help to create physical, emotional, and mental well being.

In addition to properly functioning chakras providing us with well being, they also become the connection and link to extra sensory perception. With aligned and open chakras, it is possible to experience the dimensions beyond this one. A properly functioning heart chakra can provide us with clairsentience, which is the ability to physically or emotionally feel something beyond the normal five senses. The throat chakra when properly opened and working can provide us with clairaudience, the capacity to hear thoughts and words from the spiritual world. Clairvoyance, which is clear sight, is received through a balanced and open third eye chakra. In addition, the ability of Clair cognizance, or clear knowing, can come through an aligned crown chakra at the top of the head.

There are also secondary chakras that are not as well known and are less talked about, which are located in the palms of our hands and soles of our feet. They also serve an important purpose, with the chakras in our feet providing an excellent tool for grounding our energies to Earth, and the palm chakras aiding in a person channeling light energies to others. Together the seven major chakras along with the secondary chakras provide us with tools in maintaining body well being, also strengthening the link between this side and the high realms. When they are aligned and functioning properly, they will spin their energies in either a clockwise or counterclockwise direction, appearing to some clairvoyants able to see them like spinning wheels of color.

The spiritual world conducts itself in a world of thought. Without the limitations of physical life like here on Earth, spiritual communication and travel is of course much different than done in the physical way. There is no need to speak with our mouths, and it is not required that we travel like we do in a physical body. Thoughts are things in the spiritual realm, and they are every bit as real as anything on the physical plane. We can speak with telepathy and think wherever we want to be, going there in an instant. It is possible to astral travel during sleep to a person or place on Earth, and we can also do this when we travel to the astral and heaven planes. Also, with thoughts being totally real, it is possible to make an immediate connection with our passed over loved ones after we have placed our thoughts and concentration on them. When we do this, our thoughts have traveled to The Other Side in an instant and can be felt by those we are thinking of.

Visualization becomes an important part of sending our thoughts to that side and just like thoughts; it is something very real and concrete in the spiritual world. We can mentally picture our thoughts traveling to that dimension and immediately they are there. It is possible to send our thoughts of love to a certain person in Heaven; however we must be careful in sending continuous nonstop thoughts to them. We are bound to our passed over loved ones by the bond of unconditional love. That tie can never be broken and will always be there. Unconditional love carries some of the highest energies there are. But we must remember they are living very wonderful active lives, and to constantly send them thoughts would be similar to us hearing the phone ringing over and over all day long. It is great to get a phone call, but do we want to hear the phone ringing all day when there are other activities to do? They will always love us and enjoy hearing our loving thoughts directed to them, and they will even come around us on the earth plane now and then. But they also need to go about their own lives in that high place.

Prayer is another important method of creating a link with that side, and when we pray, we are at once creating the strong connection between the two worlds. Our prayers do go directly to God with every prayer being heard. We can even communicate with the angels, asking them to be with us and to guide us. They will hear those thoughts, sending comfort and peace back to us. Prayer is a wonderful tool to connect with The Other Side, but it is always best when done with a sincere and pure heart. Since we are connecting with a realm that has extremely high energies and is perfect in every way, in order to make the best possible connection, we need to approach our communication in a genuine and heartfelt manner.

Just as it is possible to send our thoughts and prayers to the high realms, it is also possible to direct some of those magnificent energies to us. Although we live on the earth plane which has both positivity and negativity, it is still attainable to experience some of those perfect energies right here on Earth. When we connect with those vibrations, and they come down to us, it becomes possible to experience a small portion of the incredible sixth sense world of those high dimensions.

The God Light is the most rarified and highest of the energies in the high places. This light consists of the greatest brilliant gold coloring imaginable. In the psychic world, the senses tend to blend together. Because of this, it is not only possible to perceive some of the magnificent golden hues, but it also becomes achievable to feel a portion of the great depth of love that resides within that energy. This light consists of the total unconditional caring that God has for all of us, and it is energy so great we can only sense a minute portion of it after having connected to it.

Regardless of your belief system and what you envision God to be, it is possible to bring a small fraction of those brilliant energies down to your physical and spiritual being. All we have to do is ask with a sincere and pure heart, and it will be granted to us. After asking, we can direct some of these glorious energies to us by envisioning the most intense golden light possible. As this light of total goodness and purity flows toward you, humbly and gratefully accept it into the aura around you. Let it flow into your crown chakra at the top of your head, slowly filling your entire being with righteousness and light. Feel the light traveling through your body, filling every atom of your being. As you connect with the golden light in this way, let the rarified vibration of that energy radiate through your body, mind, and soul, blessing you with the feeling of great happiness and joy. Allow the energy to reach each of your chakras, enabling them to function better and allowing you to develop increased paranormal awareness. Let this light open up a greater consciousness and perception within you.

Another powerful light from the high realms is The White Light of the Holy Spirit. This energy shows itself as a brilliant white light that carries with it great healing capabilities. It can also be directed toward us in much the same way as the God Light. Just like the light of gold, this white light is there for our asking. We only need to ask with a humble heart that it enter, surround, and envelop us, and immediately it will be sent to us. Because of the pureness and brilliance of this light, it produces curative and therapeutic qualities. It can dissolve lower energies of negativity and replace them with the high energies of pureness and positivity.

When you direct this light to your crown chakra, let it flow into your body and travel throughout your being. Feel the light entering the crown chakra and moving down to every part of your body. Experience the great pureness and wholesomeness of the energy, letting the force dissipate any negativity you might be feeling at the time. You can also have this light surround you, greatly brightening your aura and strengthening your chakra energy centers. All you have to do is ask that this extraordinary energy be with you and visualize it being there. You can then enjoy the great gift of these two brilliant energies, letting them become a part of your daily life and allowing them to increase your perceptive awareness and sensitivity.

Both of these energies shine very brightly in the dimension we call Heaven, reaching out to every part and corner of that magnificent place. They shine throughout Paradise in their brilliant pure form, casting a glow of eternal love and healing everywhere. Since there are no lower energies, these energies of light are able to shine throughout the most wonderful and perfect place imaginable.

Because of the radiant energies shining throughout that high realm on The Other Side, all of the colors in that dimension are infinitely overstated compared to those on the earth plane. Every color imaginable and multitudes of colors we have never seen on Earth are in that place. The perfect gold and white energies of light create an eternal feeling of absolute bliss, harmony, and peace.

From my sixth sense experiences as a psychic, I have previously mentioned that Heaven is very close to us, and it is actually superimposed directly above the earth plane. It is mere feet above us, but in a completely different dimension than we are in. Although Earth has the combination of both lighter positive and denser negative energies, Heaven has only the awesome lighter positive energies. Although very close to each other and only several feet apart, the high realm of The Other Side is totally different and is far removed from us in energy and vibration.

I have clairvoyantly observed and felt through clairsentience the great difference between here and there. That side has the same type of topography as here on Earth. There are beautiful flowers and trees, mountains and valleys, and oceans. However, the vibrant positive energy of the place gives everything there a pristine and unspoiled perfection, as if it were created yesterday. This is the eternal world of The Other Side.

The people in that superb realm live very active and rewarding lives. Since there is no time or night on that side as we know it, they can literally stay constantly busy. They do not tire, because there are no lower energies there to tire them. The people of The Other Side eternally sense the energizing and uplifting feel of that dimension, living every moment filled with caring and joy for one another.

As you connect with these different high energies of light, feel a portion of the unconditional love and bliss that is always present on that side. Let these feelings permeate your entire being, and remember that however hard our difficulties are on this side, they can be met with the connection of pure positivity that is ever-present on The Other Side. Use that positive energy to work with your problems. It is possible to meet our earth challenges, working with them and then overcoming them with definite optimistic solutions. Have faith in these high energies, and let them be your guide to a more fulfilling and rewarding life. May the blessings of The Light always be with each and every one of you.

Epilogue

When we begin to reach out and strengthen our connection with The Light of The Other Side, fascinating things begin to happen. We begin to view life with a different perspective, realizing that the physical earth plane is only a small part of the big picture. As our understanding of this fact starts to amplify and grow; we increasingly recognize there is much more to life beyond our own dimension. When this happens, our sensitivities start to expand, and we find ourselves with greater awareness, having a new and out of the ordinary outlook on life.

Connecting with the high realms can bring much pleasure and satisfaction into our lives. There are different levels to the spiritual side, and because of this fact, it is always vital to reach for only the high energies of light. It is these high spiritual places that hold the purest of vibrations, so it is those energies of clarity and goodness that we should strive to connect with.

Earth is our special classroom, but very often life here can be challenging. We come to the earth plane to grow spiritually, and during this process of furthering our spiritual expansion, we often encounter various difficult situations. These circumstances can test our very nature, but we must remember that we come here to experience these things, and it should be our goal to overcome these obstacles.

When we fortify our connection with the high vibrations of light, we actually make it easier to face these earth challenges. The complete positivity of those rarified energies can help us face any difficulty head on, overcoming and hopefully replacing it with positive resolve. As we do this, we not only feel great satisfaction from having conquered a difficulty, but we are also furthering our own soul development at the same time.

It is an amazing universe beyond our physical Earth. Explore the sixth sense world of your spiritual side and the extra perceptive energies of The Other Side. Let The Light surround and engulf you with its goodness, expanding your consciousness and allowing it to help you with your daily life. Those energies are there for the taking. All we have to do is have the desire to increase our own personal light relationship, use that intent, and then simply connect.